Praise for *Swim or Die*

"Sharon McGroder's *Swim or Die* is an honest and thoughtful account of a mother's journey navigating a son's illness, while grappling with a genetic disease and scars from her own childhood that come back to haunt her... A beautiful story about love, family, and thriving against all odds. Inspirational!"

—**ANNA GREKA,** MD, PhD (Dr. Greka is a physician-scientist whose groundbreaking research may lead to a treatment for ADTKD, the second most common genetic kidney disease in the U.S.)

"The author details the ups and downs (of Lyme disease) that families face with amazing description, facts, and emotions. *Swim or Die* is a must-read for patients with Lyme disease and their caregivers."

—**CHRISTINE READING,** mother of a teenage daughter suffering from Lyme disease

"The real-life personal drama of a family impacted by chronic Lyme disease."

—**SAMUEL SHOR,** MD, FACP, Past President, ILADS (International Lyme and Associated Diseases Society), and Associate Clinical Professor, George Washington University Health Care Sciences

"A heartwarming read of resilience and perseverance. Sharon McGroder's memoir illuminates ways our societal systems and policies can support rather than hinder one's personal and professional journey. A timely example of the inextricable bond between parents and children and why supporting both together strengthens families across generations."

—**MARJORIE SIMS,** Managing Director of Ascend at the Aspen Institute and expert in two-generation approaches for advancing family economic security across generations

SHARON M. McGRODER

Swim or Die

A MOTHER'S HUMBLING JOURNEY
THROUGH CHRONIC ILLNESS

RIVER GROVE
BOOKS

This book is a memoir reflecting the author's present recollections of experiences over time. Its story and its words are the author's alone. Some details and characteristics may be changed, some events may be compressed, and some dialogue may be recreated. Some names and identifying characteristics of persons referenced in this book, as well as identifying places, have been changed to protect the privacy of the individuals and their families.

This book is not intended as a substitute for the medical advice of physicians. The reader should regularly consult a physician in matters relating to their health, particularly with respect to any symptoms that may require diagnosis or medical attention.

Published by River Grove Books
Austin, TX
www.rivergrovebooks.com

Copyright © 2025 by Sharon M. McGroder

All rights reserved.

Thank you for purchasing an authorized edition of this book and for complying with copyright law. No part of this book may be reproduced, stored in a retrieval system, or transmitted by any means, electronic, mechanical, photocopying, recording, or otherwise, without written permission from the copyright holder.

Distributed by River Grove Books

Design and composition by Greenleaf Book Group
Cover design by Greenleaf Book Group
Cover images used under license from ©Adobestock.com

Publisher's Cataloging-in-Publication data is available.

Print ISBN: 978-1-63299-971-9

eBook ISBN: 978-1-63299-972-6

First Edition

Acknowledgments

First and foremost, I must thank Evan for letting me tell his story—his ups and downs and his triumphant recovery from Lyme disease. Your journey from Lyme disease to graduate school for clinical mental health counseling remains an inspiration to me. Thanks also to my husband, Pete, for his undying support throughout Evan's illness and while I wrote this book. I don't know how I got so lucky. And Matthew, although you play a small role in this story, you play a tremendous role in my life. I love you all.

I am grateful to all the doctors who helped us understand the nature of Evan's illness, especially his Lyme specialist, Dr. Sultana Afrooz. Your calm demeanor and optimistic outlook were every bit as critical as your medical expertise in treating my son.

Evan would not be where he is today without the support, guidance, and encouragement of his high school principal, Dr. John Brewer; his guidance counselor, Mrs. Tana Amodeo; and the homebound instructors and staff from the Loudoun County (VA) School District. Mrs. Amodeo, you were instrumental not only in Evan's successful completion of high school but also in his choice of career, for which I will be forever grateful.

If it takes a village to raise a child, then it takes a community to support the parents. I've been fortunate to have friends, neighbors, and a church community to celebrate with in good times and help sustain me during difficult times. Allison Tracy, you are a godsend. I can't imagine life without you and your wisdom, philosophical musings, light, and joy. Karen Gardiner and Jane Koppelman, I treasure our get-togethers to hold each other up and lament about politics over cocktails; Rick and Donna, Pete and I have treasured your friendship since moving next door twenty-eight years ago; to all those who prayed for Evan and our family, especially Rev. Valerie Hayes, Rev. Jon Strand, Rev. Ann Gillespie, and all the wise women and remarkable men at the Church of the Holy Comforter in Vienna, VA, I thank you from the bottom of my heart. And to my "little" sister, Colleen McGroder: You are an inspiration, and I treasure your friendship, wisdom, and support.

To my memoir coach, Marion Roach Smith, and other experts (in particular, Lisa Cooper Ellison, Jane Friedman, Tiffany Yates Martin, Linda Joy Myers, Brooke Warner, K.M. Weiland, and Allison Williams): You helped this left-brained researcher learn the craft and the joy of storytelling, and I thank you.

To those who read and provided indispensable feedback on earlier drafts—Pete, Allison, Karen, Jane, Jordan Sher, Judith Bowers, Laura Branchflower, Trish Lockhard, Julia Scheeres, Ann Segal, and my sisters, Colleen McGroder and Sheila Montague—thank you for supporting me through this stressful, creative, frustrating, wonderful process!

An appreciative shoutout to my master class classmates—Amy, Bettina, Christine, Rebecca, Ron, and Jordan—whose Zoom faces I looked forward to seeing each month during COVID and whose feedback during our six months together taught me how to critically review my own work.

Finally, to the talented team at Greenleaf Publishing—especially editor Sally Garland, production manager Jen Glynn, and developmental editor Danielle Perlin-Good—you saw something in an early draft that led you to take a chance on me. Your support and patience through multiple rewrites over two years gave me the confidence to finish this book, and I am grateful.

The day is cold, and dark, and dreary;
It rains, and the wind is never weary;
The vine still clings to the mouldering wall,
But at every gust the dead leaves fall,
And the day is dark and dreary.

My life is cold, and dark, and dreary;
It rains, and the wind is never weary;
My thoughts still cling to the mouldering past,
But the hopes of youth fall thick in the blast,
And the days are dark and dreary.

Be still, sad heart, and cease repining;
Behind the clouds is the sun still shining;
Thy fate is the common fate of all,
Into each life some rain must fall,
Some days must be dark and dreary.

—Henry Wadsworth Longfellow, "The Rainy Day"

Contents

Prologue: February 2016   1

Chapter 1: Early March 2016   7

Chapter 2: Late March 2016   15

Chapter 3: April 2016   23

Chapter 4: May 2016   27

Chapter 5: Memorial Day Weekend, 2016   33

Chapter 6: June 2016   39

Chapter 7: August 2016   47

Chapter 8: Early September 2016   51

Chapter 9: Late September 2016   57

Chapter 10: October 2016   61

Chapter 11: December 2016   69

Chapter 12: January 2017   73

Chapter 13: February 2017   85

Chapter 14: March 2017   93

Chapter 15: May 2017   97

Chapter 16: June 2017   103

Chapter 17: August 2017   109

Chapter 18: September 2017   111

Chapter 19: October 2017   119

Chapter 20: January 2018   125

Chapter 21: March 2018   133

Chapter 22: April 2018   137

Chapter 23: June 2018   145

Chapter 24: October 2018   151

Chapter 25: February 2019   155

Chapter 26: March–May 2019   159

Chapter 27: June 2019   163

Chapter 28: October 2019   165

Chapter 29: May 2020   169

Chapter 30: September 2020   173

Chapter 31: October 2020   181

Chapter 32: Winter 2020–2021   185

Chapter 33: June 2021   189

Chapter 34: June 2021   191

Chapter 35: August 2021   193

Epilogue: Fall 2021   195

References   199

Notes   201

About the Author   203

Prologue

February 2016

Evan had just grabbed the rebound at the opponent's net, his solid 6' 1" frame towering over the other tenth graders, and was tearing up the basketball court. The sound of squeaky shoes on the polished floor echoed throughout the gymnasium as the opposing team tried but failed to catch up to him. The score was tied with only seconds left in the fourth quarter. This would be the last play of the game.

"Go, Evan!" I yelled, both a show of support and a directive.

"You got this, Evan!" hollered Matthew through cupped hands. Startled but warmed by this outburst from my otherwise quiet older son, I smiled.

"Take the layup!" my husband, Pete, coached from the stands.

And it looked like Evan was about to do just that. Except, he didn't. At the last second, without taking his eye off the net, Evan bounce-passed the ball through an opponent's legs to one of his teammates, who took the easy layup. The ball dropped into the net, and the crowd went wild. A loud buzzer signaled the end of the game. Evan's team had won on a buzzer-beater.

"Nice pass, Evan!" roared our team's parents. I looked down the silver metal bleachers at the opposing team's parents and saw stunned faces, eyes wide with disbelief, murmuring "Whoa, that was an amazing pass" and "That kid is really good."

"That's my son!" I boasted to no one in particular, beaming with pride and clapping my hands until they hurt. Standing next to me, Pete chuckled. Far from being embarrassed by my outburst, Pete seemed to relish my over-the-top enthusiasm.

Evan high-fived his teammates, then scanned the bleachers, eventually spotting the three of us. His eyes twinkled as his face creased into a wide smile, exposing his dimpled cheeks. He gave a small, almost self-conscious wave, then turned back to the celebration mid-court before heading to the locker room for his coach's debrief with the team.

Pete, Matthew, and I waited for Evan outside the locker room, the pungent smell of teenage body odor lingering in the hallway. Evan eventually emerged, combing his fingers through his overgrown, sweat-drenched hair and carrying his duffle bag. We each leaned in to give him a hug, and with our arms entwining and foreheads touching, we morphed into one big family hug. Always the last to let go, I programmed my brain to remember this moment—the strong arms around me, the boys' shaggy hair in my eyes, and the musky scent of sweat—profoundly grateful for the love I felt for and from these three wonderful people. I finally let go, and we made our way to the parking lot. The late afternoon sun was warm, taking the chill out of the crisp February air.

On the drive home, Pete, Matthew, and Evan dissected the game's plays. Pete had coached Matthew's and Evan's club basketball teams throughout elementary and middle school, and hearing the intensity in his voice, I could tell he missed it. But even if he could help coach high school basketball ball—a role reserved for school employees—I don't think he would. "The parent-child dynamic can sometimes get in the way of the coach-player relationship," Pete had reflected on multiple occasions when he and Evan had butted heads over play calls and substitutions. "And vice versa."

"Next time, Evan, puh-leeease take the easy layup!" Pete implored in mock exasperation, his hands outstretched, beseeching the powers that be. They'd had this conversation many times as coach and player, but Evan continued to pass the ball when he could have easily scored.

"But I like passing," Evan held firm. "It's fun, and it gives others a chance to score too."

Pete shook his head in defeat, but I saw the small smile cross his face, his lower lip quivering ever so slightly—a touching tell that he was actually proud of our son's selflessness.

I listened to their discussion and playful banter with delight, knowing that these ordinary interactions were actually extraordinary, and not to be taken for granted.

That evening, we enjoyed a double celebration: Evan's win and Matthew's nineteenth birthday. Matthew was a freshman at Virginia Polytechnic Institute and State University—better known as Virginia Tech. Growing up, the boys got to pick what they wanted for dinner and what flavors of cake and ice cream they wanted for their birthdays. Although their cake and ice cream preferences varied over the years—their bubble gum and cotton candy phases were especially memorable—they always requested Pete's chicken enchiladas for dinner. Pete had begun with a Betty Crocker recipe and, over the years, tweaked it to make it his own.

"Do I smell Dad's famous enchiladas?" Matthew exclaimed, the creaky stairs announcing his quick but contained descent.

Matthew was the spitting image of Pete: dark hair, the tan Alvarez skin tone, and almond-shaped brown eyes full of kindness. His lean six-foot frame masked the introverted, empathetic teddy bear within. Matthew wasn't the overscheduled teen on every sports team or in every club, and he preferred to spend his free time with family. Unlike me in high school: I joined as many clubs as possible, mostly to minimize the time I spent in my conflict-ridden home.

Evan took after my side of the family: His fair skin, hazel-green eyes, and reddish-brown hair reflected his Irish heritage. An inch taller than Matthew—a source of pride as the younger brother—Evan took the stairs two at a time, skipping the last step and landing loudly, dramatically, on the floor.

If not for their distinctive ways of descending the stairs, I might have mistaken Evan for Matthew. It was harder these days to tell the boys apart simply from their voices. Evan's deep baritone was incongruent with the toddler I still saw when I looked at him, the one obediently clutching five-year-old Matthew's hand as we crossed a parking lot, saying, "You're my best friend, Matthew."

To which Matthew had responded, "I certainly love you, Evan."

I watched both boys—young men really—jostle each other playfully as they set the dining room table, debating whether the Washington Wizards would defeat the Cleveland Cavaliers in an upcoming game.

"The Wizards have Beal and Wall. The Cavs only have LeBron," Evan asserted, confident in his opinion and never shy about challenging his older brother.

"I didn't say the Cavs would win, I just said they'd have a good chance now that LeBron is back."

The debate became more heated, their voices rising and their jostling more aggressive. My heart quickened at the sound of the commotion, fearing an escalation into violence. I knew it was irrational—my boys never fought physically—but I couldn't out-logic my thumping heart or my churning gut where my feelings of anxiety from childhood lived.

Taking a few calming breaths, I called for the boys to settle down, sounding more in control of myself than I felt.

Deftly changing the subject as we sat down to dinner, Pete asked Matthew how college was going. I admired Pete's conversational style when asking these sorts of questions; I often came across like a police officer interrogating a crime suspect. I couldn't help it, so intense was my interest in how my children were doing. I had always wanted to be a good parent—involved, supportive—and to avoid my parents' mistakes. It was a steep learning curve with many slips.

"Fine," came Matthew's monosyllabic response.

I wanted to know more, but I didn't want to come across as confrontational on this special day, so I didn't push.

Our bellies full and our plates empty, we each rinsed and placed our dirty dishes in the dishwasher. Pete brought the frosted cake into the kitchen, placed the "1" and "9" candles in the center, and lit them. We sang "Happy Birthday"—with Evan mockingly harmonizing off-key like Michael Scott in *The Office*—and Matthew blew out the candles.

While I relished Matthew's growing independence and all the "firsts" that awaited him in college and beyond, I wished that time would slow down with Evan so I could relish all the "lasts"—his last high school basketball game, his last band concert, the last time teaching our child to drive, even the last time undergoing the arduous and fraught process of applying to colleges.

Little did I know that I would soon regret making this wish because not only did time slow down, it came to a dead stop like a ship mysteriously running aground in the open sea.

Chapter 1

Early March 2016

The morning sun, low in the eastern sky, blinded me as I crossed the Potomac River into Washington, DC. I admired the Kennedy Center, the Lincoln Memorial, and the Washington Monument to my left, the winged Institute of Peace building directly in front of me, and the arched spires of the Air Force Memorial, the Pentagon, and Arlington National Cemetery to my right. I never tired of these sights; knowing they'd greet me each morning helped ease the stress of my hour-long commute from our bucolic exurb thirty miles away.

After one of the warmest winters on record, spring had arrived early. February's crocuses had given way to March's daffodils, and cherry blossoms in all shades of pink fluttered in the ever-warming breeze. The sky was a cobalt blue, not a cloud in sight.

Stopped at a light on Maine Avenue, I rolled down the passenger-side window and snapped pictures of the Jefferson Memorial on the cherry tree–laden tidal basin less than a quarter of a mile away. Drinking in the dual scents of damp asphalt and loamy soil, I reveled in the thought that Matthew would be home for spring break in two days. I made a mental note to check with my supervisor about working from home for a few days next week.

My cell phone buzzed, and I read the text from Evan.

Wednesday, March 2, 2016

> Evan: I have a headache and a stomachache. Can I stay home from school?

Evan was a good student, and he was not one to fake an illness to get out of going to school. But he was prone to psychosomatic symptoms when stressed, and he had been worried about his drop in grades since December.

> Mom: Can't u try to go? U have exams coming up. And u r already behind.

> Evan: Mom I really can't. Pls don't make me

As a child, Evan had often been uneasy in new situations and had difficulty transitioning between tasks. But with reassurance and a loving push, he eventually settled in and did what he was supposed to.

I thought of four-year-old Evan, his pudgy face damp with tears, begging to stay home from preschool. Somehow, I had coaxed him into the minivan, but he had refused to get out once we reached his preschool two miles away. Although he was capable of removing his car seat buckle, he had made no move to do so—a final show of defiance.

"Honey, you DO have friends, and they'll be glad to see you!" I had cajoled.

Evan had given a slow shake of his head, his resistance beginning to wane. His intense eyes held mine as if to say: *You better not be lying to me.*

I had opened the minivan's sliding door and instinctively swept his unruly hair from his eyes, still glassy with unshed tears. My heart ached for this nervous little boy as I unbuckled his car seat and held him close, for my sake as much as for his.

I had walked Evan to his classroom, his tiny hand clutching mine, a slight spring returning to his step. The brightly colored construction paper letters of the alphabet and days of the week chart adorning the walls made for a cheery welcome. A little boy called out, "Evan!" and ran over to hug him. Evan's teacher had reassured me that once I left, he was fine. Still, she offered to task him with updating the weather chart, and I relaxed, knowing how much Evan enjoyed placing the cutout sun or cloud or umbrella under the correct day of the week.

I had turned to leave, and Evan waved goodbye, his face set in a determined smile. My chest had tightened, admiring his effort to be brave amid his fear, however misplaced.

But today, Evan's plaintive plea felt sincere; I could picture his beleaguered face as he typed out those words.

> Mom: K. But no video games. Rest and drink water. Feel better.

A car behind me honked, and I caught up to the throng of cars creeping slowly forward.

Ten minutes later, I pulled into my usual spot in the lower level of the parking garage and trudged up three flights of stairs, pathetically proud of this intentional but insufficient exercise regimen. I swung open the glass doors to the lobby and greeted the receptionist behind the room-length desk, her broad smile a beacon of welcome that outshined even the large National Governors Association sign behind her.

The National Governors Association is a bipartisan organization of our nation's governors, and I worked in its Center for Best Practices, which sought to help state leaders adopt evidence-based practices and develop innovative solutions to today's most pressing public policy challenges. As the program director for human services policy, I oversaw a small staff responsible for convening meetings of state leaders with the goal of improving state policies and service delivery systems aimed at preventing and alleviating poverty and protecting vulnerable individuals, children, and families. I had started this job nine months ago and was pleasantly surprised that the partisan rancor that paralyzed the federal government was less prevalent at the state level—at least behind closed doors, where leaders of both parties were willing to learn about and share bipartisan solutions to common public policy challenges. The day passed in a blur of meetings, phone calls, and emails as my team and I prepared to convene over one hundred state leaders from across the country in Salt Lake City later in the month.

On the drive home, my mind gradually shifted from work to Evan. I thought about last December, when he had complained of a stomachache and had asked to stay home, right around midterms. Normally an A/B student, Evan's grades had begun to slide earlier that quarter, and by December, he had three Cs and a D in AP World History.

"I feel so bad disappointing Dr. Smith," Evan had said, clearly discouraged. "You can tell he really likes world history, and he's such a good teacher. But my mind freezes up during tests, and I can't seem to remember my homework assignments."

I had emailed his guidance counselor, Mrs. Amodeo, requesting that she meet with Evan to offer concrete advice on how to keep track of assignments and due dates. I had made a point of letting her know that Pete and I were working with Evan on time management at home—I didn't want her to think that we weren't involved parents—but that

Evan might be more open to advice coming from someone other than his mom and dad.

I had also shared with Mrs. Amodeo that Evan was disappointed about his AP World History grade and was considering dropping the course. "I told him he needs to stick it out and try harder"—I had emailed, hoping to show how much I valued personal responsibility—"and he did! After completing two projects for another class late last night, he reflected (without prompting from me) that he wished he had put that much effort into his AP World History class." Where there's a will, there's a way, I knew.

With that boost of confidence, Evan had spent the winter break resting and catching up on his history assignments, using the organizational strategies and note-taking tools offered by Mrs. Amodeo. Not surprisingly, his stomachache had quickly disappeared.

I smiled at the memory, pleased that Evan had learned about the power of perseverance.

I pulled into my driveway just as the sun was setting, turning the sky myriad shades of yellow, red, and orange against a smattering of gray clouds.

"How's Evan?" I called out to Pete as I crossed the threshold. I tossed my coat on a chair and kicked off my heels, looking forward to slipping on sweatpants, a T-shirt, and slippers.

I worked the late shift, getting the boys off to school and arriving home by dinner, while Pete worked the early shift, leaving the house at o'dark hundred so he could be home with the boys after school.

"He doesn't have a fever." Pete kissed me hello, as he had done every morning and every evening throughout our twenty-year marriage. "He says he slept all day."

I knocked softly on Evan's bedroom door.

"Come in . . ." he croaked.

I turned the knob but found the door locked, a recent development in my teenage son's quest for privacy.

"Can you get the key?" he moaned, evidently too tired to get out of bed to unlock the door.

I grabbed the key from my nightstand, then knocked again. "I'm coming in," I announced.

The blue and orange walls—a holdover from middle school when his favorite basketball team was the Oklahoma City Thunder—seemed brighter than usual. On the far wall hung team pictures from Evan's years of playing basketball, the shy smile of a second grader morphing ever so slightly over the years to the confident smile of a tenth grader.

Evan was splayed on his bed, still in the ripped T-shirt and plaid flannel pajama bottoms he wore the night before. One arm was folded over his eyes, and the other rested on his stomach, his hand gently pressing down.

"What's going on, honey?"

"My head hurts, and my stomach is killing me," he managed.

I laid my hand on his forehead. Pete was right . . . he didn't feel feverish.

I told Evan I'd be right back and returned minutes later with a cold cloth, a bottle of Tylenol, and a glass of water. I placed the cold cloth on his forehead, pressing lightly, willing his headache to go away. His deep, even breathing told me he had fallen asleep. I kissed the top of his head and set the medicine on his nightstand.

"Get some good rest," I whispered and quietly left.

Evan remained out of school the rest of the week. I debated calling the doctor, but I figured he just had a stomach bug, in which case, there wasn't much they could do. It would just have to run its course.

After work on Friday, I picked up three days' worth of Evan's missed homework assignments from the school's main office. Arriving home, I saw Matthew unpacking his car. I rushed to greet him just as Pete and

Evan came outside for our traditional group hug. Evan's face looked drawn; his Irish skin was paler than usual. But there was no mistaking his pure joy at seeing Matthew.

With Matthew home from college, Evan's mood brightened, and his symptoms appeared to diminish. For the next week, he attended school during the day and played video games with Matthew during the evening. I loved that they spent time together, but I was concerned—and annoyed—that Evan continued to fall behind in school.

Sitting down to dinner one evening, I decided to broach the issue. "Evan, if you're well enough to play video games, you're well enough to do homework." My back stiffened in anticipation of an argument.

"But my head hurts when I do homework!" Evan grumped, his voice equal parts defiance and dejection.

"Probably because you're playing too many video games." I didn't want to have this argument again, but I couldn't seem to stop myself.

Pete turned toward Evan, his voice calm. "Can you try to do a little homework every day between video games?"

Between video games? Is he serious?

"What Dad means," I glared disapprovingly at Pete, "is that you can play video games *after* you've done some homework. You're falling way behind."

"Mom, I know," he said, the anger and exasperation clear in his voice. "You don't have to keep reminding me."

Evan pushed away from the table, the chair scraping loudly against the hardwood floor, and stomped upstairs to his room, slamming the door. Matthew quietly followed him upstairs.

My shoulders hunched in defeat, and I stole a glance at Pete. Without meeting my eyes or saying a word, he carried the dirty dinner dishes to the kitchen.

I sat quietly at the dining room table, willing my racing heart to slow down. I didn't mean to be argumentative; I just wanted to convey to Evan the importance of taking his responsibilities seriously, no matter how difficult. He was too inexperienced in life to understand the dire consequences that could result if you didn't do what you were supposed to.

Chapter 2

Late March 2016

As Matthew packed to return to Virginia Tech, I packed for my work trip to Salt Lake City. The National Governors Association was launching an initiative to help state leaders develop strategies for fostering economic security across generations by helping parents secure jobs with family-sustaining wages while simultaneously supporting their children's educational success. This approach was dubbed "two-generation," and this meeting was the first of several trips I had planned to educate state leaders about the promise of two-generation strategies and to generate interest in applying to participate in this initiative. My staff and I had spent months planning for this high-profile meeting, and we were both exhausted and excited that it was finally here. Kind of like childbirth.

The flight to Salt Lake City was uneventful, restful even, as I luxuriated in the fact that there was nowhere else I had to be for the next four hours. I arrived at the hotel in the late afternoon, the sun not yet setting behind the snow-capped mountains but the long shadows suggesting that it would soon.

As I was checking in, I heard a commotion in the lobby. I turned to see about fifteen very large men in matching sweatsuits hauling gym bags onto a bus. A quick check of their logos told me that it was the Cleveland Cavaliers. I pulled out my phone and quickly snapped a picture of LeBron James and texted it to Pete, Matthew, and Evan with the caption "Look who's staying at my hotel!" I smiled as I imagined their surprised faces reading the text.

I made my way to my room and unpacked my suitcase, debating whether to find a nearby restaurant or order room service, when my cell phone rang. It was Pete.

"How is Evan?" The question shot from my mouth like a cannonball. I was feeling equal parts concerned and guilty that I was not home with him.

"Hi to you too," joked Pete. And then, "He seems okay. He's playing video games right now."

I couldn't tell if he truly was not worried, or if he was just trying to allay my concerns. Either way, I was grateful.

"Do you think he'll feel up to going to school tomorrow?" I was sitting on the crisply made king bed, running my hand over the thick comforter, smoothing imaginary wrinkles. "Between the week before Christmas and this past month, he's already missed fifteen days of school."

"I don't see why not. He made it to school all last week, and he's been catching up on his overdue assignments all day."

I felt a weight lift, yet I was suddenly exhausted, the adrenaline draining from my body. "I better run," I said, stifling a yawn. "I'm getting tired, and I still need to eat dinner."

"Good luck on your meeting. Love you," said Pete.

"Thanks. Love you too." Words not spoken in my childhood, my heart swelled at how easily we said this to each other.

Standing in front of the full-length mirror the next morning, I did a final check of my outfit: the tan suede skirt falling just above the knee, the cream-colored knit turtleneck and matching cardigan, and the brown flats. Dismayed at the dark circles only partially hidden by my tortoiseshell glasses, I considered the modestly mascaraed and lipsticked face looking back at me. Not bad for fifty-one, I decided.

I had just finished dabbing concealer under my eyes when I received a familiar text. *He must not have been able to reach Pete*, I thought, concerned that Evan was reaching out to me when I was out of town.

Monday, March 14, 2016

> Evan: I don't want to be sending this but I'm really tired and have a headache and stomachache

Not again. Uncharitably, I began to wonder if he was faking it.

> Mom: But u were fine last week. Are u just sad Matthew's gone back to school?

> Evan: Yes but that's not it. I don't feel well and I kinda want to take my spring break early. You said it yourself, I'm way behind. I just want to rest and catch up.

I glanced at the clock, which told me I was running late.

> Mom: Okay

I sighed and put away thoughts of Evan as though returning a cracked vase to its shelf—deliberately but delicately, with great care—until I had time to fix it. I grabbed my briefcase and left for my meeting.

I arrived home two days later. Quickly paying the cab driver and grabbing my bags, I walked briskly to the front door, eager to see Evan and Pete.

"Evan hasn't eaten anything, and he went right to bed when he got home from school, complaining about a splitting headache," Pete explained as he gave me a kiss and took my bags. "He looked exhausted."

I went upstairs to check on Evan. His door was locked, so I rapped softly. "Honey, can I come in?"

"Mmmphh."

I grabbed the key from my nightstand and let myself in. The lights were off, the room-darkening shades were drawn, and the floor fan was slowly oscillating toward and away from the lump of covers on the bed. I approached Evan, and my heart ached for my whiskered boy. I instinctively brushed the hair from his eyes and cupped his cheeks in my hands.

"Your hands are cold. That feels good."

I couldn't tell if he had a fever or if he was warm from his many layers of blankets.

"Can you press my head?" he murmured, his face etched in pain.

"Your headache's bad, huh?" I gently but firmly pressed his temples.

"Yes. It's pounding," he whimpered. "Worse than ever."

"Does light or sound make it worse?"

"Yes. How did you know?"

"It sounds like a migraine. I'm taking you to urgent care."

"Mom, no . . ." he murmured. "Just let me sleep. I'll go tomorrow."

I deliberated for a minute, but then his light snoring told me he had drifted back to sleep. I slowly removed my hands from his head, careful not to wake him—the same way I used to stop rubbing his back when he was a baby and quietly sneak out of the nursery.

Pete was doing the dishes when I entered the kitchen.

"Wow, Evan is really sick."

"I know. I guess we know he's not faking it."

I glanced up, wondering if that remark was aimed at me or if he unknowingly revealed the shame I felt for doubting Evan.

Normally, I would have been grateful for a sunny spring day, but not today. Evan cowered as he stepped outside, shrinking from the light as if the sun were physically burning him. He crawled into the front seat of the car for the short ride to urgent care and immediately covered his eyes with both hands. I made a mental note to buy him sunglasses.

Ten minutes later, I stood at the self-serve check-in kiosk while Evan lumbered to the back of the waiting room to a chair away from the wall of windows. He collapsed into the seat, still shielding his eyes. With only one other family in the lobby, a pink-faced toddler cuddled on her mother's ample lap, I hoped it would be a short wait.

No sooner had the mother and her feverish-looking child been taken back, a second nurse called Evan's name, her sad smile conveying sympathy as she watched Evan slowly hoist himself from the chair and walk unsteadily to the door she held open.

The back room contained about a dozen examining rooms, six to the left and six to the right, with the doctors' offices, a lab, and an X-ray room against the back wall. The nurse guided us to the closest examining room, directing Evan to sit in the straight-backed chair where she took his vitals. Wrapping the stethoscope around her neck, she said the doctor would be right in, then disappeared with a flourish, swishing the curtain shut behind her as if performing a magic trick.

Moments later, the curtain swished open, and the urgent care doctor entered. He was a large man, his solid stature conveying confidence and trustworthiness. He introduced himself, then asked Evan to describe his symptoms. With great effort, Evan mentioned the stomachache and the increasingly frequent headaches that did not go away with over-the-counter medication. Concluding that Evan was suffering from a migraine, the doctor offered a Toradol injection to quickly reduce his pain.

Ugh, not a needle. I looked at Evan, wilted and cringing in pain, and my mind flitted to a memory from twelve years ago.

Seven-year-old Matthew was chasing four-year-old Evan around the house. Down the front hallway, through the kitchen, rounding the dining room into the living room, and back into the hallway. Our black terrier, Punky, had joined in, barking happily as the horseplay began to escalate. "Settle down!" I had warned from the kitchen. Suddenly, I heard a blood-curdling howl. Pete and I bolted into the living room and saw Evan clutching the gash on his cheek carved by the corner of the piano bench, blood spilling between his chubby little fingers. "I'm-sorry-I'm-sorry-I'm-sorry!" Matthew had cried, explaining that he didn't mean to push him *that* hard.

We had whisked them into the car and rushed to the emergency room. They took us back immediately. "He will need a few stitches," the doctor had said. Evan heard this and began lashing out in all directions, kicking at the nurses trying to hold him down, yelling, "Get away from me, you stupid doctors!"

"Can't you hold him still?" the doctor had scolded us through clenched teeth, clearly miffed at our child's noncompliance. Pete and I had numbly obliged, and the nurses placed Evan—still screaming—in a straitjacket, allowing the doctor to proceed with the stitches. I watched in horror as they tied the jacket behind Evan's back, his pink face wet with tears showing both rage and sheer terror. Feeling horribly complicit in this betrayal, tears welled up in my eyes, even as I wondered, *Why is Evan making this so hard on himself? Why can't he just do what the doctor says?*

I returned my attention to the urgent care examination room. The doctor was describing Toradol's side effects, but I was still looking at Evan, his eyes pleading for help.

"Let's do the shot," I declared.

Moments later, a nurse entered to draw his blood and administer the Toradol. To my surprise, Evan barely winced, as if any show of pain required too much energy.

"Is it working?" I asked Evan after a few minutes.

"I think so."

Uttering the words that would become my mantra, "On a scale of one to ten, how bad is the pain?"

"About an eight."

"And before the shot?"

"An eleven," he said with a wan smile, referencing my husband's favorite *Spinal Tap* joke.

Funny kid, even in pain.

As we waited for blood work results, Evan lay down on the examining table, a glimmer of relief on his face that he no longer had to hold himself upright in a chair. I turned off the overhead lights. Thankfully, the room was cool; heat intolerance was a new, quirky symptom. *Good choice of music*, I thought, giving myself over to the airy flutes and melodic harps. *And not too loud*. Evan was nearly asleep when the doctor reentered with the test results.

"Well, Evan tested positive for mono but negative for the Epstein-Barr virus, which is the most common cause of mono. So, I don't think he has mono."

It was the first of many contradictory findings I would come across as we sought to diagnose and treat Evan's illness.

"His vitamin D is on the low side, so he should be taking a supplement," the doctor continued. "If his headaches persist, you may want to see a neurologist. Otherwise, just make sure he drinks plenty of fluids and gets lots of rest."

Evan's got the rest part covered; I need to push the fluids.

In the end, Evan was diagnosed with low vitamin D, migraine with aura, and "other fatigue"—which technically was a symptom, not a diagnosis. But it had a diagnostic code, which allowed the doctor to bill my insurance, so I forgave the misnomer.

The effects of the shot were minimal and short-lived, and Evan's migraine returned with a vengeance within days. As recommended, I made an appointment with a neurologist. I also made an appointment with a gastroenterologist; Evan's stomach pain had grown so severe he was barely eating. And just to be thorough, I also made a "sick child" appointment with Evan's pediatrician for the following day. Satisfied that I had covered all bases, I returned my focus to upcoming work deadlines.

Chapter 3

April 2016

When the boys were younger, I favored nurse practitioners, who encouraged me to trust my instincts when I noticed something ever so slightly "off" about my boys, which on one occasion led to the early detection of pneumonia in one-year-old Evan's lungs. "You heard that?" the radiologist had asked incredulously, looking at the barely visible spot on the lung X-ray. I was proud of my maternal instincts, which were once disregarded by one pediatrician who had lectured me on being a working mother and putting my baby in day care, where he determined Evan most likely had caught an infection.

On this particular day, the pediatrician we saw asked Evan all the usual questions regarding his headaches and stomachaches, and in the end, after looking at the blood work, said, "It's not mono, pneumonia, or strep. And it's not Lyme disease. I also tested for celiac disease and *H. pylori*, which is a type of bacteria that attacks the lining of your stomach and can cause pain and ulcers. But those came back negative too."

"So, what do you think it is?" I asked. "He's had these symptoms since March."

"He's probably just fighting a virus." He turned toward Evan. "Make sure you drink lots of water and get some rest."

The magic of water and rest. Maybe I would learn more from the neurologist and the gastroenterologist?

But the gastroenterologist only ruled out celiac disease, and the neurologist ruled out neurological dysfunction after Evan passed a series of memory and cognition tests and simply prescribed Imitrex and Medrol for Evan's migraines.

I began to wonder why I made these doctors' appointments at all. Surely, there was a reason why Evan was suffering from migraines and stomachaches and was always tired. I was convinced that the doctors were missing something, that their exams and blood tests had become so routine that they failed to think outside the box about what might be wrong with Evan. They seemed satisfied simply to rule out what it was not, as if that solved the problem.

It finally dawned on me: Despite the negative diagnosis from Evan's pediatrician, I was convinced that Evan had Lyme disease.

Fifteen years ago, I suffered from extreme fatigue and brain fog. At the time I was a sleep-deprived working mother with two children under the age of five, so I had just thought that was par for the course. After casually mentioning my symptoms to my chiropractor one day, he encouraged me to get tested for Lyme disease.

"But make sure you go to a Lyme-literate doctor," he'd said.

He had told me that most doctors know very little about Lyme disease, so they simply followed the CDC's two-step testing protocol, which first required a positive or equivocal result on a blood test that screens for the presence of antibodies (proteins produced by the body's immune system that bind to harmful substances, like bacteria, so they can be eliminated from the body) before following up with the more sensitive Western blot blood test. The problem is, if the screening test comes back negative, the more accurate Western blot test is never conducted, which could lead to missed diagnoses. My chiropractor had referred me to his Lyme doctor, who put me on a regimen of rotating antibiotics and immune support supplements after I tested positive for Lyme disease. After three months, I was better.

"Evan, I'm pretty sure you have Lyme disease."

"But my pediatrician said I didn't."

"I'm guessing he was following CDC protocol: He did the screening test, and when it came back negative, he didn't do any more testing. He's a great pediatrician; he's just not trained in diagnosing Lyme disease."

I pulled out my phone and googled the name of my Lyme doctor and was crestfallen to learn that he had retired. I turned to Evan, my jaw set in determination.

"We need to find you a Lyme specialist and see what they say."

Chapter 4

May 2016

The bright-orange furniture in the reception area stood in stark contrast to my mood. I stared blankly into the gray afternoon, listening to the light rain tickle the window on this unusually cool May morning. With his elbows resting on his knees, Evan gripped his head with both hands and pressed on his temples.

After a few minutes, Dr. Afrooz entered and led us to the examination room. A stout woman, her round face and smiling eyes peeked out from her brightly colored hijab. She introduced herself, and Evan shook her hand, his lanky frame towering over her. She giggled at the height difference.

"Tell me what's been going on."

"Uh, I have a migraine, and my stomach hurts," Evan began, shielding his eyes from the fluorescent lights.

"How long has this been going on?" Dr. Afrooz asked, her empathy evident as she reached over and turned off the overhead lights.

"Uh . . . a while," Evan managed.

The pain and exhaustion etched on Evan's face told me that he was in no condition to have this conversation. I filled Dr. Afrooz in on Evan's symptoms and our trips to various doctors. I pulled out the composition notebook labeled "Evan," in which I had written down the names and dosage of the migraine medicine administered by the urgent care doctor and prescribed by the neurologist and when Evan began taking them, all of which I now recited.

I put down the notebook and looked at Dr. Afrooz, who stopped typing and met my eyes.

"I had Lyme disease," I told her. "So even though his pediatrician ruled it out, I began to suspect that Evan might have it. I know that Lyme disease is your specialty, so that's why we're here."

Dr. Afrooz nodded. She grabbed her stethoscope and listened to Evan's heart and lungs.

"Did you see a tick on him, or a bull's-eye rash?"

Did I? Have we ever checked our boys for ticks? "I don't think so . . ."

"That's not surprising," she replied. Her kind eyes conveyed sympathy, not judgment. "The black-legged tick—the one that carries the bacteria that cause Lyme—is the size of a poppy seed, and they often bite where it's hard to see. Behind the knee, on the scalp, in the groin area."

Dr. Afrooz felt the lymph nodes in Evan's neck, then asked to see his back.

"Have you seen this?" Dr. Afrooz pointed to the pink striations running from side to side across his lower back. "Do you know how long Evan has had these markings?"

His ribs were clearly visible, and I was stunned by how gaunt Evan was. Once a healthy 167-pound basketball player, he now barely tipped the scales at 147 pounds. My stomach lurched.

"I did notice that. I thought they were stretch marks from his growth spurt." I paused, reflecting. "But now that I think about it, I remember being surprised that he would still have stretch marks a couple of years after his eighth-grade growth spurt." I bit my lower lip, and tears pricked my eyes, mortified I hadn't realized this earlier.

"It's a rash from a *Bartonella* infection, also called cat scratch fever. Ticks that carry the Lyme bacteria can also carry other bacteria, viruses, and parasites."

"So, Evan has had Lyme disease for a while, then?" I asked, incredulous.

"It's possible. Symptoms can emerge anywhere between six and thirty-six months after the original infection."

My throat constricted at the thought of bacteria multiplying throughout Evan's body undetected for months, possibly years.

She turned to Evan. "I'd like to get a better sense of how you've been feeling, in addition to headaches, stomachaches, and fatigue. Do you have night sweats?"

"Yes."

"Dizziness or loss of balance?"

"Yes."

"Difficulty concentrating?"

"Yes . . ."

Dr. Afrooz continued to read off symptoms, and Evan agreed to most of them—including symptoms I didn't know he was suffering from. A wave of guilt washed over me. Had Pete mentioned that Evan was having difficulty concentrating, and I just forgot? Or maybe I was so distracted by work that I wasn't really paying attention?

"Evan, you never told me you had difficulty concentrating," I said, sounding both surprised and, to my dismay, accusatory.

"I said it was hard to do schoolwork, and it's because I can't concentrate. That's why I like playing video games. I don't have to think. And it distracts me from the pain."

I sat quietly, processing what he had just told me.

"From what you've described and my clinical assessment," Dr. Afrooz began, "I believe that Evan has Lyme disease. I'd like to order blood work to test for Lyme and other coinfections. It takes two weeks to get the lab results back, so you can wait for the results, or we can start treatment immediately."

"Let's start treatment," I declared without hesitation. I turned toward Evan. He looked relieved, but I could tell that this two-hour appointment was taking its toll.

Dr. Afrooz prescribed antibiotics for the Lyme disease, probiotics to improve Evan's gut health, and supplements to support Evan's immune system, and she recommended calorie-rich drinks to help Evan gain weight. I scribbled her instructions in my notebook, barely keeping up.

"And have Evan do 23andMe. The genetic testing will show if he has any gene variants that can affect his ability to get better. Variants in the MTHFR gene, in particular, are important in Lyme patients because that gene directly affects the body's ability to get rid of toxins."

I wrote down "23andMe" and "MTHFR gene," then closed my notebook. My brain was full. I was not absorbing any more information.

"Let me see Evan in four weeks, and we'll see how he's doing." Dr. Afrooz turned toward Evan, her eyes squinting into a smile and her voice soothing. "Don't worry, Evan. I've seen lots of Lyme patients, and they've all gotten better."

I felt encouraged as we got into the car. At least now I had answers, and I could focus on what I needed to do to help Evan get better. I glanced over at Evan cowering with discomfort in the passenger seat. If the diagnosis and plan for treatment brought him any relief, it didn't show.

"When I had Lyme disease," I ventured, "my Lyme doctor put me on rotating antibiotics, and after three months, I was all better. So don't worry—you'll be fine by the time school starts in the fall. We just need to get you through the rest of the school year."

Evan continued to stare down, rubbing his head, his beleaguered body slumped against the car door window.

"At least you'll have a good essay for your college applications!" I consoled, trying to sound upbeat.

Evan said nothing.

Maybe optimism was a luxury for those of us not in constant pain.

"How is Evan feeling?"

Evan's guidance counselor sat across the small table in the windowless conference room that once may have been a closet. Her dark, shoulder-length hair framed her young face, her bangs drawing attention to her compassionate brown eyes. It had been five months since Mrs. Amodeo helped Evan with study tips and organizational strategies, back when I thought Evan's illness was stress related.

"Not well. We're pretty sure he has Lyme disease. He doesn't feel able to attend school, and his doctor agrees."

Mrs. Amodeo leaned forward attentively. "I'm so sorry to hear that."

She explained that the school district permitted homebound instruction for any student who was unable to physically attend school due to illness or injury and that this short-term arrangement, lasting up to nine weeks, would carry him through the end of the school year if necessary.

"That sounds perfect. How does it work?"

"Homebound instruction is offered only for the four core subject areas: math, English, science, and social studies," she began. "Evan will be assigned a homebound instructor for each class who will visit him for two hours every week to review his homework and work on the lessons covered in class. The homebound instructors will coordinate with Evan's teachers so that they're clear on what to focus on each week."

"What about Spanish and band?"

Evan played the tuba, and he really enjoyed it. I could still see my proud but nervous fourteen-year-old playing the tuba solo from The White Stripes's "Seven Nation Army" at the high school football game, at which eighth-grade band members were invited to play in the stands alongside the high school band. I swallowed hard to clear the lump in my throat.

"He will need to do his best to finish those up on his own." Dipping her head slightly, she sounded almost apologetic. "I'll let those teachers know what's going on and see if they can be flexible on assignments and due dates without compromising the scope of the course."

I felt my shoulders relax, not realizing I had been clenching them. I finished jotting down next steps and due dates, then closed my notebook. Mrs. Amodeo reached her hand across the table to shake goodbye, and I grasped it with both hands and gave it a squeeze.

"Thank you." My voice, trembling with both gratitude and sadness, was barely above a whisper.

I filled out the required paperwork, obtained Dr. Afrooz's signature certifying Evan's need for homebound instruction, and dropped it off at the school district headquarters. Two weeks later, the request was approved. We had a path forward.

Chapter 5

Memorial Day Weekend, 2016

Before we knew just how sick Evan was, Pete and I had planned a romantic getaway to Asheville for Memorial Day weekend. I had heard so much about this hip town nestled in the Blue Ridge Mountains of North Carolina: the vibrant music scene, the converted warehouses housing local artists in the River Arts District, amazing restaurants, creative microbreweries, and, of course, the great outdoors.

I had been looking forward to this trip, but now I wondered if we should postpone it.

"Evan will be fine," Pete reassured me. "He'll be sleeping most of the time anyway."

"But I'm afraid he won't eat or take his medicines if I'm not there to remind him." I nervously picked at a hangnail.

"Matthew's home from Tech, so Evan won't be alone. And you need a break. It's only for a few days."

A few days away can feel like an eternity when you're caring for someone who's sick. "Okay," I relented, immediately ambivalent about my decision.

Pete and I had always traveled well together, our conversations punctuated by comfortable silences, the music on the radio an opportunity for me to sing along and for Pete to mangle the melody and invent new lyrics. Laughing boisterously at his improvisation, I almost didn't hear my cell phone ring. Looking at the screen, I saw it was Dr. Afrooz, and the laughter died in my throat. I quickly answered, putting her on speakerphone.

She confirmed Evan's Lyme diagnosis and informed me that Evan's blood work also showed signs of multiple fungal infections. I quickly scribbled notes on whatever pieces of scrap paper I could find, then thanked her for calling and hung up.

I called up a web browser on my phone and, with fumbling fingers, typed in the names of the infections Dr. Afrooz mentioned.

"The Mayo Clinic says that aspergillosis is a fungal infection that usually affects the respiratory system. *Aspergillus*, the mold that triggers aspergillosis, can be found everywhere and is usually harmless."[1]

My eyes darted down the web page, knowing there had to be bad news.

"But it can cause serious illnesses in people with weakened immune systems . . ." I turned to Pete, a look of panic on my face. "Evan's immune system is compromised thanks to Lyme disease!"

Like the sudden onset of storm clouds in a cerulean sky, I felt tricked into believing it was going to be a good day. Next, I typed in "hypersensitivity pneumonitis."

"WebMD says, 'Normally, the immune system—your body's defense against germs—causes inflammation in your lungs as it clears away the things you're allergic to. After a while, the inflammation stops. But in some people who are hypersensitive, the lungs stay inflamed . . . and scars may develop, which can make it hard to breathe normally.'"[2]

Eyes wide, I turned to Pete. "Should we go home?"

"Do you want to?"

"I don't know! I feel like I should be home with him."

"Would it help him get better?"

I marveled at how calm he was. "Maybe . . . ?"

"He's already taking the necessary medicine, and Matthew's there if he needs anything." Pete reached across the console and placed a gentle hand on my knee. "Why don't we just enjoy the weekend and call Dr. Afrooz as soon as we get home? It's probably not as bad as it sounds."

Pete was my rock. When I was anxious, he was the balm that soothed. Although the day still felt gray, Pete had me believing it would brighten, and my pulse slowed.

"Okay. Let's have a nice weekend, and we'll deal with this when we get home."

We pulled up to the B&B in the early evening, the fading daylight conveying a sense of peace, a time for rest. The old Victorian home was a buttery shade of yellow, its wide porch with a half-dozen Adirondack chairs a beacon of welcome. The house had been divided into apartments; our B&B was on the top floor. Pete and I carefully lugged our suitcases up what I assumed was the original staircase with its ornate wooden handrail and shallow steps meant for shorter people. The house smelled old, which at first felt comforting, nostalgic even, until I realized that the musty odor was a sure sign of mold and mildew.

I thought of Evan. Was he like this house, appearing sturdy on the outside but decaying on the inside from an invisible microbe? I shuddered and, pushing the image from my mind, insisted that we call Evan, interrupting Pete's unpacking.

I dialed our home number and put my phone on speaker.

Matthew picked up and told us that Evan was sleeping and had been sleeping most of the day. "Yes, he ate something . . . Yes, he took his medicine . . . Yes, he's drinking water," he replied to my quickfire queries. Pete rubbed my back if to say: *See? Evan is in good hands.*

We chatted for a few more minutes until Matthew said he really should get back to his video game; his friends were waiting.

"Love you," the three of us said in unison.

I slept fitfully that night. Images of bugs filled my dreams, and I woke up several times throughout the night to find myself frantically scratching at my arms and legs.

The next morning, Pete and I grabbed cups of coffee and egg sandwiches from a nearby café, then drove ten minutes to Asheville's River Arts District. We knew we had arrived when we saw long-abandoned warehouses covered in street art—cartoon characters, elaborate portraits of famous people, and stylized graffiti. We stopped to snap pictures, then continued down the dusty road alongside the French Broad River for about a mile to what appeared to be a little village, with restaurants occupying old rowhouses and small industrial buildings containing the working studios and galleries of over two hundred artists.

We parked the car and spent the next several hours popping in and out of several studios. One artist used foil in her mountain scenes that glittered in the light, creating a vibrant, otherworldly feel. Another artist posted signs on his creations that required a double take, inviting visitors to "Please touch!" the bumpy globs of paint and found objects protruding from the canvas. Clearly, I'd been neglecting my right brain, which drank in these elixirs of beauty. I thought of the metaphor of placing the airline mask on yourself before assisting your child, and my ambivalence about this trip faded.

Over the next two days, Pete and I enjoyed cocktails on the Sunset Terrace of the famed Omni Grove Park Inn, whose views of Blue Ridge Mountains—rows upon rows of peaks melting from clear green in the foreground to hazy blues farther west—were the most beautiful I had ever seen. We ate dinner at a Caribbean-style restaurant in the historic residential neighborhood of Montford, where Pete indulged in mahi-mahi served with mango salsa and a locally brewed stout, and I sipped a local IPA alongside a pasta dish with a creative array of vegetables in a creamy white sauce. We went ziplining, sailing side-by-side above the forested slopes of Pisgah National Forest at sixty miles per hour.

I returned to work after the Memorial Day weekend feeling rested and ready to dive back in. As the lead for the National Governors Association's two-generation initiative, I was facing a number of upcoming deadlines and long hours over the next few months. I thanked Pete for convincing me to go to Asheville.

Chapter 6

June 2016

The hotel meeting room was small, intimate even, with its acoustic-tiled drop ceiling and soft carpet with geometric patterns in pleasing shades of green and blue. The room was blessedly cool, a comfortable contrast to the sweltering afternoon heat that the locals didn't seem to mind but that I, as a visitor to Kansas City, found unbearable for June.

I looked out at the audience: two dozen state agency directors responsible for administering the federal Temporary Assistance for Needy Families (or TANF) program, also known as "welfare."

"States interested in more efficient ways to meet the interrelated, often complex needs of families with low incomes are considering two-generation approaches to provide appropriate, coordinated, and seamless services to both the adults and the children in those families," I began.

These leaders from ten Midwestern states listened expectantly as I described the ways they could use their TANF programs to place parents—and, consequently, their children—on a pathway to economic security. I treasured the underlying assumption of two-generation approaches that, like any parent, those with low incomes simply wanted what was best for their children; they just had more limited opportunities and resources to make it happen. In this era of partisan bickering—amplified by this year's especially divisive presidential election—it felt good to work on a policy issue that both Democrats and Republicans could agree on, and one that was deeply important to me.

My mind drifted, as it often did in my professional life, to my childhood and to what led me down this career path.

We were a typical, lower middle-class, Irish-Catholic family living outside Buffalo, New York, in a post war suburb reminiscent of Bailey Park from the holiday classic *It's a Wonderful Life*. My father, the breadwinner, worked as a salesman at a box manufacturing company, and my mother was a stay-at-home mom—literally. We had one family car, and my father used it for his short commute to and from work.

My parents had four children in four years: my two older brothers, then me, then my younger sister, born eleven months later—my Irish twin. The eldest, Brian, was born in 1961 on my mother's twenty-third birthday. The medical staff wouldn't let my mother see Brian for two days, cautioning my father—who had been allowed to see Brian—that she would be hysterical when she learned that Brian had Down syndrome. Doctors told my parents that Brian would never read, write, or learn like a "normal" child, and they advised institutionalizing him. I don't know if it was their faith in God or pure Irish stubbornness, but my parents ignored their advice. There was a five-year hiatus after my Irish twin, and then my parents had two more children in close succession—my "little" sisters.

My childhood home was full of music. My mother played the piano, and I'd watch her slim fingers dance gracefully across the keys as she played Beethoven's "Für Elise." My father sang—the Steve Conway classic "Daddy's Little Girl" was my favorite. We read *Highlights* magazine together most evenings before bedtime. Like others in our predominantly Catholic community, we ate fish on Fridays and went to Mass each Sunday.

One of my earliest memories was a professional photo session in our small living room when I was about four years old. The crisp, white linen covered a makeshift bench that held us four older children. My cupped hands were arranged just so on my juniper-green crushed velvet dress. My brothers had matching buzz cuts, blazers, and bow ties. My Irish twin, a pudgy toddler with red curls, was adorable in an impossibly white romper. The patient photographer told us to look this way and tilt our heads. My parents stood behind the photographer, miming a smile. It all felt magical.

And then it began to fall apart.

I don't know if it was the emotional stress of having a child with special needs, or the financial stress of having so many mouths to feed, or my father's increased drinking. At the first sound of a brewing argument, my Irish twin and I would retreat to our cubby-hole attic and look through binders of wallpaper samples for home projects discussed but never undertaken. We pretended we were grown-ups picking out wallpaper for each room of our fancy homes. I especially loved the fuzzy, avocado-green fleur-de-lis pattern that I would rub like a talisman until it wore thin. Late-night arguments were followed by mornings that appeared normal—breakfast before school, my father getting ready for work, sometimes even kissing my mother goodbye—but the unresolved conflict from the night before hung in the air like smoke, making it similarly hard to breathe.

By the time I was ten, my parents' arguments had become physical. One evening, recognizing the familiar rise in their voices signaling another argument about money, I heard a scuffle. I arrived in the kitchen to see my father pinning my mother against the wall, holding her hands at her sides. She was yelling at him, desperately trying to break free.

"Call the police!" my mother yelled to me.

My father looked at me. "Don't call the police," he said calmly.

I didn't know what to do. Was my mom in danger or just having a temper tantrum? Was my dad trying to hurt her or just trying to calm her down? I was frozen by fear and indecision.

"Stop, please!" I whimpered desperately, realizing I would disobey a parent either way.

As the years went by, physical conflict was replaced by a deafening silence between my parents. They finally divorced in 1979, just before my fifteenth birthday. Gloria Gaynor's "I Will Survive" topped the music charts, and *Kramer vs. Kramer* was playing in movie theaters. The divorce plunged us into poverty. It was simple math: Child support did not replace a salary, and my father's salary could not support two households. So, with her college degree in math, my mother enrolled in night school to become a tax accountant. My siblings and I watched her leave the house three nights a week in her sensible heels and modest dress with her head held high, and I thought, *Look at her! Going all Gloria Gaynor and proving she could survive!* We older siblings embraced our new responsibilities in her absence, making dinner and caring for Brian and our little sisters, who were now seven and eight years old.

But the cost of schooling had been more than we could afford, so my mother went to work as a carpenter's apprentice, assisting the family friend who had built the addition to our small house years earlier. She loved being a carpenter—a simple laborer, just like Jesus. At the end of the day, she would regale us with stories of workmen catcalling to her and her responding playfully by striking a sexy pose in her denim painter's pants and work boots. We would laugh as she reenacted the scene, one hand on her hip, the other on the back of her head, sashaying around the living room. *Maybe everything would be okay after all?* I dared to hope.

But the carpenter job had not paid well, and we older siblings started getting into mischief—going to high school parties and hanging out at a local park on weekend nights drinking beer—so my mother quit. "I have a job," she'd said. "Looking after you kids."

With no paycheck and insufficient child support, things had become dire. There were mornings without breakfast and nights when we had toast for dinner. We ate government cheese, drank powdered milk, and received free lunches at school. When the power was shut off, it was time to pay the electric bill. When the bank sent threatening letters, it was time to pay the mortgage. When it came to paying bills, my mother joked about "robbing Peter to pay Paul." I know my mother was simply trying to remain positive, but I didn't find the humor in any of this.

Thankfully, my dad's father paid our mortgage, or we would have lost our home. Food stamps helped keep us fed, and a federal home energy assistance program for low-income families kept the heat on during the cold Buffalo winters. We older siblings wanted to get jobs, but my mother refused. "Doing well in school is your job," she'd said, adding for us daughters, "Don't rely on a man. Go to college and get a good job." I held tightly to those words of wisdom like a drowning person clinging to a life preserver.

I had excelled in high school, and with the help of scholarships, federal grants, work-study, a part-time job off campus, and the maximum in student loans, I was able to attend the prestigious University of Rochester, a ninety-minute bus ride away. In my junior year, I discovered that the university offered a master's degree in public policy, designed to equip graduates with the knowledge and skills necessary to evaluate the effectiveness of programs and policies. My heart pounded with excitement as I applied, enthralled with the possibility of finding out what worked in trying to move families from poverty to economic security. I was accepted into the 3-2 program, which allowed me to obtain a master's degree with only one additional year of schooling by taking master's-level classes in my senior year that also counted toward my political science major.

Nearing graduation, I applied for and was awarded an internship with the federal government. I packed up my meager belongings and moved to Washington, DC, to work in the US Department of Health and Human Services, where I oversaw research projects and helped to develop federal policy relating to child care, Head Start, and welfare reform. The job had been a natural fit for me, with my academic background and my firsthand experience with poverty and social services programs.

Eventually, I wanted a more in-depth understanding of how parenting and family functioning affected child development, so after five years, I quit my job to attend graduate school full-time. I obtained a PhD in human development and family studies from Penn State University, then returned to DC, where I spent the next twenty years studying family strengthening programs in various policy research firms and advising federal officials on programs that supported both family economic security and child well-being. Just over a year ago, a former colleague recruited me to join her at the National Governors Association Center for Best Practices.

I returned my attention to the convening of state leaders and, with renewed conviction and a sense of urgency, extolled the promise of two-generation approaches for lifting families out of poverty and encouraged these state leaders to apply for the National Governors Association's two-generation initiative being launched in the fall.

"When are applications due?" asked a well-dressed gentleman in the back of the room during the Q&A session.

"The funding announcement will be released next week, and applications will be due at the end of July. We'll select states by the end of August and begin working with those states starting in September." I sighed to myself. Another summer that felt over before it had barely begun.

A few minutes later, the meeting adjourned, and after thanking the meeting host, I took the elevator up to my hotel room. Mentally exhausted, I collapsed on the king-size bed, sinking blissfully into the soft down comforter.

I could easily have fallen asleep for the night. Instead, I kicked off my shoes, propped myself against the fluffed cluster of pillows at the headboard, then called home.

"Cold cloths and headache medicine seem to be taking the edge off his migraines," Pete said, anticipating my concerns. "And he's getting lots of rest."

"And his stomachaches? How is his appetite?"

"He's eating egg sandwiches and other bland foods. He's also trying every day to get some homework done," Pete reported, the calm in his voice conveying that all was well.

Although the school year had ended two weeks ago, Evan had not completed his tenth-grade courses, so the school district had arranged for Evan to continue homebound instruction through the summer.

"And how are *you*?" Pete asked. "How did the meeting go?"

"It went well." I rubbed the back of my neck. "I'm fine . . . just tired."

Pete and I talked for a few more minutes—he told me about his day, and I reminded him of my flight information—then said goodbye.

"I love you. Give Evan a kiss for me. See you tomorrow."

I hung up and turned to look out the window. The stately buildings of downtown Kansas City were backlit by the late afternoon sun. I wished I had the energy to explore, to walk around the neighborhood or grab a taxi to a popular hot spot offering authentic Kansas City barbecue. But I just wasn't feeling it. Although the sun had not yet set, my day was done. I took a shower, put on my pajamas, ordered room service, and turned off my brain for the night.

Chapter 7

August 2016

As I anticipated, summer passed in a blur. The occasional ten-hour day became more frequent as I struggled to meet deadlines for the two-generation initiative, only to come home for my second shift of taking care of Evan. Pete picked up much of the slack at home, leaving work earlier and taking the lead on making dinner most nights, while I organized Evan's medications, reviewed his blood work results, managed communications and appointments with his doctor and his guidance counselor, and encouraged/cajoled Evan to take his medicine and keep up with his schoolwork.

We also had to figure out how Evan would undertake eleventh grade.

I reached out to Evan's guidance counselor requesting that we meet to discuss accommodations that Evan would need to attend in-person classes in the fall, and by mid-August, we had a plan. Evan would take only four courses—AP US and Virginia History, English 11 Honors, Chemistry, and Precalculus—with two classes each day. Mrs. Amodeo had arranged it so that Evan's classes met midday, allowing him to arrive later and leave earlier to avoid the noisy crush of classmates. I had been so overcome by Mrs. Amodeo's thoughtfulness that I had flung myself at her at the end of our meeting and wrapped her in a tight hug, trying but failing to convey the depth of my gratitude.

Today, as I stared out of the floor-to-ceiling windows of the executive conference room overlooking the US Capitol, the maple trees performed a languid dance in the late-afternoon August heat, and I felt their sluggishness. *Has Evan eaten today? Has he taken his medicine?* My stomach tightened with worry. If only I were home to make sure he did what he was supposed to.

"Sharon, what do you think?"

Hearing my name dragged my mind back to the conference room. The air conditioning clicked on, causing my arms to prickle with goosebumps. At the front of the room stood an empty podium adorned with the National Governors Association logo, flanked on either side by floor plants in colorful ceramic pots, their shiny, healthy-looking green leaves a testament to someone's loving care. Probably the secretary, I decided, and I made a mental note to thank her.

Seated around the perfectly centered table were my coworkers, project partners, and foundation funders, and they were staring at me expectantly. We had just spent the last eight hours weighing the pros and cons of each state's application for the two-generation initiative, and I was mentally exhausted from facilitating that discussion. After months of hard work, we were finally ready to select the states to participate in this high-profile effort, and my colleagues were waiting for me to weigh in.

What do I think? With all eyes on me, I suddenly realized that I couldn't think. I couldn't form a coherent thought—about anything. My hands began to sweat, and my breathing became shallow.

"Can we take a break?" I managed in a breathless voice.

Without waiting for an answer, I headed to the restroom and splashed cold water on my face. Looking up, I barely recognized the stranger in the mirror, her sunken eyes and the dark circles suggesting a serious lack of sleep. *Pull it together*, I admonished my haggard reflection. *We're almost done!* After a few steadying breaths, I returned to the conference room. With great effort, I forced Evan from my mind and presented my recommendations, backing up my selections with a coherent rationale. Less than an hour later, the group agreed on a path forward, and we adjourned for the evening.

It was after 6:00 p.m. when I unlocked my car and collapsed into the driver's seat, still fuzzy headed and drained of energy. I started my car and wound my way up to the parking garage exit, growing dizzier with each turn. I swiped my ID, the mechanical arm lifted, and I slowly drove out. Approaching a streetlight, I braked—panicked. Suddenly, I couldn't remember whether green meant stop or go. What had been second nature for thirty-five years now required the concentration of a newly-licensed driver. Please, God, let me make it home safely, I prayed. What is wrong with me?

With a white-knuckle grip on the steering wheel and painfully intent concentration, I managed to make it home unscathed. Physically, anyway.

Chapter 8

Early September 2016

I hadn't told Pete about my brain malfunction at work; I knew it was just stress and that I would be fine. Besides, I had more important things to worry about.

Despite the reduced schedule, Evan missed the entire first week of eleventh grade, plagued with migraines each morning. On the couple of days he had managed to get out of bed, he'd barely had the energy to shower. On Friday, he'd actually made it to the front door. But as he turned to leave the house, his body had folded along with his resolve, faced with the daunting task of walking the five minutes to school. I had offered to drive him, but if he couldn't walk to school, he'd said, with equal parts scorn and weariness, how would he manage to walk from class to class?

The following week, Pete and I met with Mrs. Amodeo to discuss options. I had wanted Evan to join us so that he had a say in his schooling, but he'd said he didn't feel up to it.

"I suggest he drop Chemistry," Mrs. Amodeo began after we settled ourselves in the small conference room, now decked out with a coffee maker on a small end table in the corner. "It's a lab course, and if he can't come to school, then he can't do the lab assignments." A pause, then, "But don't worry! He can take it next year as a senior."

Next year. Certainly he'd be back to in-person classes by then, wouldn't he? I refused to consider any other scenario.

"Okay . . ." Pete said, then turned to me, his brows raised, seeking confirmation. We had already discussed reducing Evan's courseload prior to this meeting, so I simply nodded absentmindedly, still lost in thought.

"And because of the workload in AP courses, I suggest he take the regular eleventh-grade history course instead."

"That all sounds good," I agreed. "Can we also go back to homebound instruction?"

Now at the end of his second week of school, Evan still had yet to attend one class. He had been contacting his teachers daily to request class notes and homework assignments, which I then picked up from school on my way home from work. By now, the front office staff knew who I was, and upon seeing me enter the building, they had the accordion file folder labeled "Evan" ready before I'd even reached the reception desk. Keeping up with assignments had been hard enough for Evan, but trying to teach himself the material from class notes and handouts was nearly impossible.

"Of course," Mrs. Amodeo said, giving a small smile. She handed us the Parental Request for Homebound Instruction and the Physician Certification of Need forms, as she had in May.

It occurred to me that I might want to Xerox these forms for future use, just in case.

"Severe fatigue prevents patient from being able to attend school; persistent headache adds to debilitating nature of patient's condition," Dr. Afrooz had written on the physician certification form, justifying the need for homebound instruction.

Debilitating.

I reflected on that word as Evan and I sat in Dr. Afrooz's waiting room, the familiar orange chairs eliciting annoyance rather than cheery comfort, as if a promise had been broken. Evan wasn't just sick; he was debilitated. I knew that—I'd *seen* it—but this word conjured images of decay . . . and death.

Dr. Afrooz entered, interrupting my ruminations, and led us to the examination room. She took Evan's blood pressure and temperature, felt the lymph nodes in his neck, donned her stethoscope to listen to his breathing, then looked at his latest blood test results.

"Evan has secondary infections," Dr. Afrooz began, so-called because they occurred as a result of Evan's weakened immune system. She was particularly concerned about the mold test results.

"Evan tested positive for mycotoxins," Dr. Afrooz said, looking up from her notes.

"Mycotoxins?" I murmured. I had been so preoccupied trying to figure out how Evan would undertake eleventh grade that I had forgotten to review Evan's latest blood test results before this appointment.

"Mycotoxins are toxic substances produced by fungi. They are typically found in the environment but can quickly reproduce in animals and humans."

Wait, what? Fungi were colonizing Evan's body and releasing poisonous substances?

I looked over at Evan, who continued to stare out the window into the gray day. I couldn't tell if he hadn't heard her or if he'd just grown accustomed to bad news.

I was beginning to realize that it was misleading to say simply that Evan had Lyme disease. It was more accurate to say that he had "numerous tick-borne and secondary infections," but it was just easier to say he had Lyme disease.

"Evan?" Dr. Afrooz's voice was always gentle but no more than in this moment. "Can you tell me about your symptoms this month?"

Walking through the checklist of symptoms, Dr. Afrooz newly diagnosed Evan with ataxia (poor muscle control, as evidenced by Evan's difficulties with balance), cervicalgia (neck pain from inflammation of joints), and encephalopathy (a change in brain functioning that causes neurological symptoms such as confusion and an inability to concentrate).

Dr. Afrooz turned to me, her kind smile conveying sympathy but also confidence.

"I'd like to start Evan on IV medicine."

That caught Evan's attention. He and I exchanged confused looks.

"The longer an infection goes untreated," she explained, "the longer it takes to get better—sometimes twice as long. Given we're in the fifth month of treatment, Evan had likely been infected for ten months or more by the time you came to see me in May. I believe he needs stronger medicine."

"Is that done at the hospital?" I picked at a hangnail.

"No. Evan will do it at home. A PICC line—that's a peripherally inserted central catheter—will be surgically inserted into a vein in Evan's upper arm, where he'll connect the bags of antibiotics and antifungals. A nurse will come to your home to show him how to do it, then she'll return for weekly blood draws to monitor how Evan's body is tolerating the medicine and to make sure everything is going okay."

More needles. Evan looked over at me, his eyes wide with fear.

Evan said nothing during the appointment or on the drive home, and I wondered what he was thinking. I felt the urge to tell him that everything would be okay, but I wasn't sure I believed that myself. So I said nothing.

We pulled into the driveway. With great exertion, Evan pushed the car door open, lumbered to the front door, and dragged himself up the stairs to his room, the *creak-slam* of his bedroom door echoing throughout the house.

I collapsed on the front porch step, still numb with the news that Evan would need a tube surgically implanted into his arm to self-administer bags of medicine three times a day for the next six to nine months to kill not just the Lyme bacteria but also a mold infestation releasing poisonous substances into his body.

The late afternoon sun threw long shadows on the front lawn, like sentries keeping watch. I prayed for the cathartic release of a good cry, but no tears came. Instead, my chest ached as if the unshed tears had found their way to my lungs, stealing my breath and pressing on my heart.

With a heavy sigh, I hoisted myself off the front step and made my way inside. I grabbed a glass of red wine and collapsed on the sofa.

Before long, our dogs began barking, signaling that Pete had arrived home from work. I greeted him at the front door with a kiss and an update on Evan's appointment, my voice quivering as I described the PICC line surgery and self-administered IV treatments Evan would need.

"What are we going to do?" I searched Pete's face for an answer, even though the obvious solution was staring us in the face.

Since my brain had shut down last month, I'd been working from home as much as possible so that I could be there for Evan. Now that we had selected the states for the two-generation initiative, all that was left to do was assign staff to each state and set up protocols for how they were to engage with state leaders around helping them design their two-generation efforts. Like a long-distance runner spotting the finish line, I knew that my race was almost over, that moving this initiative forward no longer rested solely on my weary shoulders. And with Evan's illness being worse than we thought, I knew I couldn't keep pushing forward on both fronts. Something had to give.

"Do you think one of us should be home with him?" he asked in reply.

In my thirties, the thought of being a stay-at-home mother terrified me. *What if Pete and I divorced, like my parents did?* But now, twenty years later, I was not worried about falling into poverty, and I was confident in the strength of my marriage . . . and also in my ability to support myself financially, if necessary.

And Evan needed us now like never before.

"I'm happy to stay home with him," I declared without hesitation.

"Are you sure?" Pete asked. "I could stay home if you want."

My sweet husband, a true partner. I crossed the room and enfolded him in my arms. "I got this," I reassured Pete. "I could use a break from work anyway. The long hours are killing me."

I think we also knew that, between the two of us, I was the more proactive, outspoken advocate who would research the hell out of this disease and not rest until we found the answers we needed and the treatments that would work.

Chapter 9

Late September 2016

It was clear that I needed to learn more about Lyme disease beyond my own short-lived experience. So, on this crisp Saturday morning, with Evan still sleeping and Pete mowing the lawn, I grabbed my "Evan" composition notebook containing questions and answers from our appointments with Dr. Afrooz and began at the beginning.

I logged into the patient portal to take a closer look at the results of Evan's blood tests to date. As I suspected, Evan's pediatrician had conducted the screening for Lyme disease—the first step in the CDC's two-step diagnostic protocol—which had come back negative, so he never conducted the second step, the Western blot.

Dr. Afrooz had conducted both the screening and Western blot blood tests back in May. The screening test result came back negative, while both the Western blot IgG and IgM test results came back as having "possible clinical significance." Lyme tests are imperfect, Dr. Afrooz had explained, in large part because they don't detect the presence of the actual Lyme bacteria but only the antibodies produced by the immune system in response to infection. But the problem was that the corkscrew-shaped Lyme bacteria not only suppresses the immune system, it outsmarts it by outrunning white blood cells and cocooning itself inside a sticky biofilm, making it difficult to detect by the body's immune system. As a result, immune-response blood tests like the Western blot could result in false negatives. That's why the clinical assessment of symptoms was paramount, she explained. With suggestive results on both the Western blot IgG and IgM antibody tests, coupled with Evan's symptoms, it had been easy for Dr. Afrooz to conclude that Evan had Lyme disease.

Next, I opened my browser and typed, "Lyme disease."

The website for the Centers for Disease Control and Prevention, or CDC, explained that "Lyme disease is caused by the bacterium *Borrelia burgdorferi*. It is transmitted to humans through the bite of infected blacklegged ticks. Typical symptoms include fever, headache, fatigue, and a characteristic skin rash called erythema migrans (EM) that resembles a bull's eye."[3]

This I already knew. I continued to read.

"If left untreated, infection can spread to joints, the heart, and the nervous system."

I paused, not sure I read that right. I knew about joint pain, but infecting the heart and nervous system? I had never experienced that; I didn't even know that was possible. My pulse quickened, and I prayed we had caught the infection in time to prevent its spread to Evan's organs and his nervous system. I took a deep breath and pushed away the dark "what if?" scenarios that began to creep into my consciousness.

Preferring to solve problems rather than to perseverate over them, I opened a new tab, and with the cursor blinking at me expectantly, I typed: "how to treat Lyme disease."

The standard treatment endorsed by the mainstream medical community was ten to fourteen days of an antibiotic, typically doxycycline.

But things got complicated when the telltale bull's-eye rash is not seen—which the CDC said happens in twenty to thirty percent of all Lyme patients[4]—making it nearly impossible to tell how long someone has been infected. The short course of antibiotics had been shown to be successful in treating recently infected patients, but there was disagreement over how to treat patients for whom the standard treatment didn't work, a condition referred to as chronic Lyme disease or Post-Treatment Lyme Disease Syndrome (PTLDS). Some experts insisted that those suffering from PTLDS did not, could not possibly, still have Lyme disease and that their PTLDS symptoms are due to other infections. Others surmised that, for some, Lyme disease triggered an autoimmune response that accounted for long-term symptoms. But a growing minority of Lyme-literate health-care professionals believed that patients could, in fact, still be suffering from Lyme disease after completing the standard treatment and that longer-term antibiotic use coupled with holistic health therapies was warranted. Such were "the Lyme wars."

Next, I looked for books on how to treat Lyme disease.

I was drawn to a particular title, *Why Can't I Get Better? Solving the Mystery of Lyme and Chronic Disease*. I thought sardonically, *I've always loved a good mystery.* "Dr. Richard Horowitz has treated thousands of patients with tick-borne illness and has conducted research on both traditional and integrative approaches to treating Lyme disease," read the blurb.[5] Bingo. I added it to my cart, hoping to learn about all available treatment options.

By the same author, I saw *How Can I Get Better? An Action Plan for Treating Resistant Lyme & Chronic Disease*. In this follow-up to his earlier book, I was told I would find "the latest pertinent information on the most important scientific discoveries; emerging research on bacterial 'persisters'—bacteria that can survive antibiotics—and new therapies to get rid of them; and a seven-step action plan that patients and doctors can follow to ensure better health."[6] Yes, an action plan! That's what I needed. I clicked "Add to Cart."

A third title caught my eye: *The Lyme Diet: Nutritional Strategies for Healing from Lyme Disease,* written by a naturopathic doctor specializing in Lyme disease. "People who have suffered for many years recover best when they utilize a comprehensive approach, especially one that includes optimal nutrition," the description promised. "This book provides sound, thoroughly researched information presented in a clean and cogent format."[7] They had me at "thoroughly researched." I added it to my cart.

Those three books should keep me busy for a while, I thought, as I typed in my credit card information, arranged for overnight delivery, and hit "Place Order."

A mystery indeed. But I was a detective, confident that I would find the answers.

Chapter 10

October 2016

Homebound instruction was not the godsend it had been in May. Throughout September, we continued to cancel appointments with homebound instructors as Evan found it harder and harder to get out of bed. As a result, he fell further and further behind in all of his classes. I was at my wit's end trying to figure out how Evan could manage school, and I feared that it was only a matter of time before he gave up altogether—on school, and on life.

"Evan can take all of his classes online." Mrs. Amodeo offered, her brown eyes creasing with sadness when we met for the third time in as many months. She offered me a cup of coffee, which I accepted. This tiny conference room was starting to feel like my home away from home.

"That would give him the flexibility to do his assignments when he's feeling up to it," she continued. "And it wouldn't require teachers to come to your home."

That certainly would be easier for Evan . . . and it would eliminate the arguments he and I had each time he refused to come downstairs for his lessons.

Mrs. Amodeo leaned forward, her elbows resting on the faux-wood board table. "But I suggest he try to come to school for at least one of his courses. That way, he can see his friends."

I agreed that was a great idea. In addition to his buddies on the basketball team, Evan had a posse of four close friends who had done everything together since middle school. They'd go to the movies, hang out at a local playground, or order pizza and play Mario Kart in one of their basements. Evan hadn't seen these friends or anyone from school since he had begun homebound instruction in May, and Pete and I were worried about his growing isolation.

That evening, I updated Pete and Evan on the meeting with Mrs. Amodeo.

"Ev, you can take all of your courses online, but Mrs. Amodeo thought it might be good if you took one class in person at school so you can see your friends." Despite his insistence that he couldn't handle in-person classes, I had hoped that the lure of seeing his friends while committing to only one in-person class, meeting only two or three times a week, might appeal to him.

Evan looked doubtful, shaking his head before I had even finished. "But what if I don't feel well and can't go?" Before I could answer with words of encouragement, Evan cut me off. "Do you know how hard it is not wanting to go anywhere or do anything because I never know how I'm going to feel?" he shouted, glaring at me.

Evan's lower lip trembled as he tried to regain his composure. Stunned into silence by his outburst, I looked over at Pete, who was already walking toward Evan, his arms open to embrace him in a hug. Until that moment, I hadn't realized that Evan feared uncertainty as much as, if not more than, any microbe assaulting his body. I joined their hug, my entire body aching with sorrow as Evan sobbed quietly into Pete's shoulder.

The next day, I notified Mrs. Amodeo that Evan would be taking all four of his eleventh-grade courses online.

Pete had just taken the chicken enchiladas out of the oven when the doorbell rang. Our dogs, Champer and Brady, began barking as they skittered to the front door. Setting down the oven mitts, Pete shooed our dogs away and opened the door. His parents entered, smiling, their arms loaded with wrapped presents and plastic grocery bags, which we knew were full of bags of M&Ms and other sugary treats that were on sale at the commissary near their home.

"How's Evan?" Pete's mother asked, setting the bags on the kitchen counter and looking around for him.

"He's not having a good day," I answered, giving her and Pete's father a hug. "He's resting in his room."

"But he'll come down later?"

A simple question, but not a simple answer.

"I hope so."

Just then, our three- and five-year-old nephews burst through the front door, shouting, "Happy birthday, Evan!" Behind them, Pete's sister and her husband entered, apologizing for their boys' rambunctiousness as they wrestled with wrapped presents, a bottle of wine, a diaper bag, and the car seat containing their sleeping baby.

I relieved them of the brightly colored packages and bottle of sauvignon blanc and led them to the sunroom at the back of our house. Our nephews were already climbing on top of Matthew, who had been sitting quietly looking at his phone and was now trying without luck to calm them down.

"Where's Evan?" they shouted in unison, bouncing up and down on tippy-toes, unable to contain their excitement.

"In his room," Matthew answered and seemed to immediately regret his response as they scampered past him toward the stairway, chanting, "Wake him up! Wake him up!"

"Hey, guys?" I intercepted them, restraining them with a hug. "Why don't you play outside while I check on Evan?"

"I call the slide first," the five-year-old declared, doing an about-face and jostling past his younger brother toward the sunroom and out the door to the playground in our neighborhood's common area that lay beyond.

I missed the days when my children were so easily redirected and compliant.

With a sad smile, I climbed the stairs and tiptoed to the end of the hall. "Evan?" I knocked quietly on his door. "Can I come in?"

The bedframe squeaked, followed by the thud of footsteps as he stood up, walked to the door, and let me in.

"The family is here." An obvious statement, given the loud hullabaloo taking place downstairs. "Do you want to come down?"

"I'm really tired," he replied, crawling back into bed.

"How about coming down later for cake and ice cream?"

"Maybe." He rolled over, signaling that our conversation was over.

I returned downstairs, trying to engage in the festivities, hoping no one asked any more questions that I didn't know the answers to.

An hour later, with salsa-and-cheese-encrusted dishes soaking in the sink, I approached Evan's door. "Ev, we're ready for cake and ice cream . . ." I left the rest unsaid, as if not asking the question meant he couldn't say no.

Evan opened the door, his hair unruly, his bleary eyes suggesting I woke him up. "I'll come down for a bit."

Thank God. These days, I took victories wherever I could find them.

He took a step and immediately lost his balance. I rushed to catch him, my arms spread wide, but he was able to right himself by leaning against the wall. His bouts of dizziness were becoming more frequent, and I feared that one day I wouldn't be there to catch him. I shook the thought away and gently took his arm, guiding him carefully down the stairs.

"Evan!" cheered his cousins, aunts, uncle, and grandparents. I couldn't help but think of Norm from *Cheers*, and I managed a smile. I also embraced humor whenever I could.

Evan walked unsteadily into the sunroom and took his place at the head of the table, his eyes squinting in the bright sunlight. After enduring an off-key rendition of "Happy Birthday," he blew out the candles with the help of his young cousins and made the traditional first cut into Pete's homemade chocolate cake. While others indulged in cake and ice cream, Evan opened presents and read the birthday cards out loud, his voice hitching slightly when trying to decipher the crayon sentiments of his cousins wishing him both "happy birthday" and "get well soon!" With his guest-of-honor duties complete, Evan said thank you and hugged each family member goodbye. I helped him upstairs to his room, where I tucked him in, kissed his forehead, and wished him a good night.

An hour or so later, Pete and I waved goodbye to our last guests and closed the front door.

I dropped my sweater and laptop in my office, grabbed my mug, and made a beeline for the kitchen. Today's the day, I thought, my palms sweating as I stared at the coffee machine. I decided to treat myself to a high-calorie concoction instead of my usual black coffee as a small comfort for what lay ahead.

Nodding "good morning" to my staff as I hurried past their cubicles, I entered my office, closed the door, and took a seat at my desk. I swiveled toward my computer . . . and smashed my knee on the hidden file cabinet, muffling an obscenity. *It's going to be that kind of day. At least it's Friday*, I consoled myself. I turned on my computer and began sifting through emails, but my mind was elsewhere.

I hadn't yet told my supervisor that I was resigning, and I dreaded letting him know. I knew he would understand—he knew Evan had been sick since spring, and he had been supportive of my need for a flexible work schedule—but like most nonprofit organizations, the National Governors Association was sorely understaffed, and it felt irresponsible to leave just as the two-generation initiative was getting off the ground. Pete finally convinced me to rip off the bandage and tell him today, giving my supervisor the weekend to process the news.

I replied to a few high-priority emails, then glanced at the artsy wall clock that matched the blue-and-brown throw rug and "Live-Love-Laugh" wall art that I had bought at Walmart in an effort to make my office feel homier. It was time, I decided.

I walked down the hall and knocked on my supervisor's half-opened door. He smiled and motioned me to come in. His L-shaped desk was immaculate, its shellacked surface containing only a lamp, phone, computer monitor, and a pad of sticky notes. I slowly lowered myself into the chair opposite his desk, my heart pounding. His smile turned quizzical, his eyebrows knitted, clearly detecting something wrong in the insincere smile pasted on my face.

"Hi, boss." I heard the apology in my voice. Then after a long pause, "You know that Evan has Lyme disease."

Leaning forward, placing his elbows on the desk and clasping his hands under his chin, he nodded, his eyes sympathetic. He seemed to know where this was going.

"Well, he's not getting better—he's getting worse, actually—so I need to be home with him." Then, to be clear, "Full-time."

His face went slack with . . . what exactly? Disappointment?

"I'm so sorry, Sharon. Of course, you need to do what you have to."

I breathed a sigh of relief, grateful for his understanding. He left the door open to my returning once Evan was better, but because I had no idea when that might be, I told him he should probably look for a replacement.

We agreed that I would work part-time, mostly from home, through the end of the calendar year to help ease the transition of my responsibilities to my coworkers. This drawn-out exit also allowed me to keep my family's health insurance until the end of the calendar year, which was critical given that we were close to meeting our $5,000 annual deductible. With my accrued sick days and vacation days, plus unpaid Family and Medical Leave, I was able to remain employed with at least some income through December.

For the next three months, I worked from home while caring for Evan and went into the office only when in-person meetings were necessary to brief others on my projects, to hand over files, and eventually, to clean out my office.

Chapter 11

December 2016

Toting a duffle bag over his shoulder and clutching his laundry basket overflowing with clothes, Matthew arrived home for winter break. The mid-December chill snaked its way inside the open door as Pete and I hugged him hello. Evan teetered down the stairs, thin and off-balanced, his smile at seeing Matthew not the least bit diminished. Matthew dropped his bags in the front hall, and his eyes zeroed in on the thick orange sock, its toes cut off to form a sleeve, that protected Evan's PICC line. A shadow crossed Matthew's face as he hugged his brother, carefully avoiding contact with Evan's wrapped arm. Releasing him, Matthew's eyes wandered to the living room where Evan's IV pole stood solemnly next to the wingback chair.

As we all made our way to the family room, Matthew leaned toward me and whispered, "Why didn't you tell me Evan was so sick?" His tone conveyed concern, not anger.

"We didn't want you to worry."

Matthew was an empath who felt things deeply and worried about those he loved. In every family photo, Matthew's arm was draped protectively around his younger brother's shoulders.

"You don't have to fill me in on everything that goes on at home, but you could have updated me on Evan. The IV was kind of a shock. Is he okay?"

I tried to ease his mind about Evan, assuring him that Evan was getting the best care possible and that he should be feeling better after the IV treatment was completed in the spring.

"So he's basically a patient 24/7? That sucks."

"Yes, it does," I agreed, reflecting on his observation.

I had been viewing Evan's illness as something that was preventing his forward progress in school and in life. But if I saw him as a patient twenty-four hours a day, seven days a week? Then I'd have to admit that he may not move forward for some time—and I wasn't sure I was ready to accept that.

Christmas Eve arrived, and Evan told us that he wouldn't be joining us at Pete's parents' house. I wasn't surprised; his migraines seemed to be worse than ever. Still, I was crushed that he would miss the festivities.

Evan loved the Alvarez Christmas Eve family tradition: His grandparents' small kitchen table overflowing with bags of M&Ms and Lindt chocolate truffles, plates of homemade cookies of every kind—the butter cookies shaped into wreaths sprinkled with green sugar and adorned with a single cinnamon button were his favorite—and a bowl of warm pigs-in-a-blanket. The roast beef dinner with all the fixings. The adults sipping eggnog spiked with Bailey's Irish Cream during the wild rumpus of opening presents. The camaraderie of same-age cousins, the engaging conversation and playful banter with his aunts and uncles, and the endless games of Mario Kart with his young cousins on an old—Evan would say "retro"—Sega Genesis console. Evan didn't even mind when Grandma asked him and all the grandchildren about their grades, reminding them of the importance of doing well in school.

Well-practiced in tag-teaming, I offered to stay home with Evan so that Pete could enjoy his family's celebration. I didn't mention that I preferred a quiet house to the fun-but-exhausting Christmas Eve festivities.

With Evan resting in bed, I kissed Pete and Matthew goodbye and settled on the couch with my dogs, my favorite gaming apps, and a glass of wine, looking forward to the temporary calm they would bring—loosening my taut muscles, slowing down my ragged breathing, and dulling my mind just enough to quiet my racing thoughts.

Eight months of navigating Evan's illness amid political upheaval was taking its toll. More and more these days, I felt my brain shutting down like it did that day in the conference room. Pete would ask me a question, and I would have to close my eyes just to concentrate on his words and their meaning. Everything was louder than usual too: voices, doors closing, the dogs' nails on the hardwood floor. I'd jump at any sudden noise. Even the sound of the running dishwasher—which usually brought comfort, reminding me of the rare times growing up when things felt orderly—churned my insides. In the middle of a conversation, I'd have to close my eyes and cover my ears to stem the overstimulation and rising aggravation I felt. It was easiest to avoid people altogether by retreating to my bedroom, closing the door, and curling up in bed. So that's what I did. Often.

Chapter 12

January 2017

I was officially unemployed.

At first, I wasn't sure what to do without the umbilical cord of emails and the shackles of a schedule dictating my daily tasks. I felt both free and aimless. Eventually, my days began to have a predictable rhythm.

I'd wake without an alarm and lie in bed, considering whether to give into the temptation to go back to sleep or let the lure of caffeine get me out of bed. I'd brew a cup of coffee, pour it into a favorite mug—today's was a gift from a friend who thought I could use a reminder from Oscar Wilde that "life is too important to be taken seriously"—and hold the warmed ceramic against my chest to melt the creeping anxiety also beginning to wake. I'd make my way to our small family room, maybe light a fire in the woodburning fireplace, and settle myself into the rickety glider rocker once used to lull my babies to sleep. With my cup of coffee in one hand and my cell phone in the other, I'd check Facebook to see what was going on outside my four walls, yearning to engage with people and issues of the day like I used to.

This morning, I saw a flurry of posts from friends, former colleagues, and parishioners from my church who planned to attend the Women's March in Washington, DC, at the end of the month, and I decided to join them. I was deeply concerned about the disrespectful treatment of women, the complete disregard of facts and science, and the antagonism bordering on bullying on full display from our new president.

It felt like everything I had taken for granted—my children's health, their bright futures, and our basic rights as citizens of the United States of America—was slowly slipping away, and it terrified me. It was as if the day-to-day anxiety I felt about Evan's health and his future was also playing out at the national level, adding to my sense of dread. I took a gulp of coffee, swallowed back tears, and pushed away the sadness and anger that threatened to drown me. I'd inevitably shut down Facebook feeling more upset than when I had logged in.

Throughout the morning, I'd listen for the sound of creaky floorboards upstairs and try to intercept Evan between his bedroom and the bathroom to see if he wanted anything to eat. Usually, I'd arrive on the top landing in time to hear the click of the lock on his bedroom door. Pursuing my stealthy kid, I'd walk down the hall and knock on his door, but before I could even form a question, Evan would cut me off with, "Yes, I'm fine . . . I just want to sleep . . . No, I don't need anything . . . Just leave me alone," his monotone voice not quite masking his impatience. Some days I'd reply with something like "Geez! Bite my head off for asking!" Other days I'd simply sigh and return to my mug of tepid coffee, deciding it was unreasonable to make it about my hurt feelings.

By 10:00 a.m., I'd remove one of the bags of IV medicine from the refrigerator so that it would be at room temperature by the time Evan got up. Too cold, and the medicine was slower to drain and almost painful entering Evan's bloodstream. But left out more than two hours, the medicine would go bad and need to be thrown away.

I'd retake my seat, cocoon myself in a fuzzy throw blanket, and open the parent portal to see how much progress Evan had made on his classes the day before. First, I'd check Evan's attendance. Online students were required to log in at least five days each week; failure to do so would count as an absence, and like in-person school, students who were absent more than fifteen times in a school year risked being unenrolled. I was pleased to see that Evan had logged on yesterday; he already had five absences for the semester and could scarcely afford another.

Next, I'd check Evan's progress. To remain on track for completing their coursework by the end of the semester, online students were encouraged to complete at least one hour-long lesson each day for each course. For Evan's two courses, that meant two hours per day, or ten hours per week, of online learning—which didn't sound unreasonable, but for Evan, that was a tall order.

Today, I scanned the "minutes spent" column for each course and was pleased to see that Evan had spent an hour yesterday working on assignments. Still, that was one hour less than recommended, which I knew would be pointed out in the weekly email updates Evan and I received from his online teachers and the school district's homebound instruction liaison. Despite the positive tone of those emails—sympathizing with how difficult it must be for Evan and congratulating him on any progress he made—they only served to remind Evan of what he already knew: No matter how hard he tried, he continued to fall behind.

Finally, I'd check Evan's grades. He was earning As and Bs on the lessons that he completed; he was simply behind in the number of lessons completed.

At 11:30 a.m., when the bag of medicine had been out for an hour and a half, I'd climb the stairs to wake Evan.

"Evan, you need to get up and do your IV."

"I'm too tired."

"Then I'll bring the medicine and your IV pole up here so you can still rest. But you need to start your IV in the next half hour."

"Mom! You know I don't like schedules or planning!" he shouted through the closed door.

"Yeah, well, things don't get done if you don't plan!" I shot back.

He'd struck a nerve. I sympathized with his situation, but I refused to believe he was helpless. I expected him to be responsible, to push through difficulties like I did when I was his age. Like sharks who needed to move forward constantly to live, "Swim or die" was my life's motto.

"You need to take your medicine on schedule, or it won't work!" I continued. *Was that true? It must be . . . why else was there a dosing schedule?*

"You only talk to me about medicine and doctors' appointments," he griped as I heard him get out of bed.

"Yeah, well, on days I barely see you, then yes, the bulk of our conversations will be about your illness!"

Evan spent most days by himself, either doing homework or resting in his bedroom or playing video games in the basement. Some days, I wondered why I had even quit my job. But then I reminded myself that being a parent wasn't always about interacting with your child—so-called "quality time." It was about simply being there in case you were needed. Which was especially true for a chronically ill child.

With a heavy sigh, I went downstairs to make sure the necessary supplies—latex gloves, alcohol wipes, surgical mask—were waiting for him on the dining room table. I heard Evan flump down the stairs. He looked pale, thin . . . nothing like the vital teenager tearing up the basketball court he'd been a year ago.

I greeted him with a hug, and he hugged me back. We pulled back, and I stared at my whiskered boy; his warm eyes and furrowed brow showed both love and frustration. I suspected he saw the same expression on my face.

I thought I was being firm—a good parent. But what did I know? The supportive parenting I had received as a child evaporated when I was a teenager amid my parents' heated divorce and the pressures of financial stress. My father became physically absent and my mother emotionally absent. Motivated by a burning desire to have a healthy family of my own one day, I studied parenting in graduate school and learned that the best parenting style for most children was authoritative parenting—characterized by both "responsiveness" to the child's needs and "demandingness" that the child follow rules.

The problem was that I found it difficult to be responsive to Evan's needs when he wasn't doing what he was supposed to. And yet, I knew he was in constant pain. How would I feel if I had a nonstop migraine for months? I decided I was being harsh and tried again.

"Honey, I know it's hard for you. I wish your illness would just go away, but it won't. We have to try different things until we see what works."

"I know," he said gently. "But it's the way you come at me with so much information on why I need to do something and what will happen if I don't. Dad is more casual, like, 'How about you do this now?' It makes me want to do what he's asking."

I felt my cheeks redden with a rising anger. *It's easy for Dad to play clean-up batter after I've loaded the bases*, I thought uncharitably. Yes, Pete was more conversational in his requests, but he also made it sound like taking medicine or doing homework or getting enough sleep was optional—only if Evan wanted to. No wonder Evan wanted me to be more like Pete. But one of us had to be firm, had to push Evan to be responsible, and as usual, that task fell to me.

I stopped myself and took a deep breath, taking Evan's hands in my own. "Okay, listen, I'll try not to overwhelm you or push too hard, if you'll really try to do what you need to."

"Mom," he said, looking me square in the eye, "I always try."

Like a surgeon with his tray of life-saving tools, Evan took stock of the supplies laid out on the dining room table. He donned his surgical mask, unwrapped an alcohol wipe, cleaned the opening of his PICC line, flushed it with a syringe of saline, then connected the bag of antibiotics that would hunt down and kill the Lyme bacteria hiding throughout his body. I winced at the slight tug on his PICC line, and Evan offered a comforting smile. He maneuvered the IV pole to the wingback chair in the living room and sat, tethered to the liquid lifeline for the next two hours.

I brought Evan a sandwich, sliced apples, and a baking cup holding ten of the forty pills he took every day, which included probiotics, antibiotics, antivirals, antifungals, antioxidants, and supplements to support gut health, mitochondrial functioning, and inflammation of the joints. It was getting to the point where I knew which pill was which simply by its size, shape, and color.

I had recently revised his meds schedule so that he didn't have to take any more than ten pills at one time. That was no simple task. I had to consider not only the dosage and frequency but also which medications were to be taken with a meal or at a certain time of day. The antibiotics and probiotics had to be taken at least two hours apart so that they didn't cancel out each other's effects. On the days when Evan rolled out of bed at 3:00 p.m., I had to decide whether to give him his morning pills or his noontime pills, then figure out what that meant for dosing the rest of the day. Some directions were so specific and impractical that noncompliance was almost inevitable. "Add fifteen drops to four ounces of water and drink thirty minutes before meals" and "Take with a teaspoon of peanut butter between meals." Evan never knew when, or even if, he was going to feel like eating. *Thank goodness I'm organized*, I consoled myself, embracing the calm that came from transforming chaos into order.

As Evan ate, I slipped upstairs to refill his seven-day pill container.

On the AM side, I had written "Wakey-Wakey" and on the PM side "Nighty-Night," hoping that Evan managed a smile each time he saw these silly phrases. I was about to flip the lids open when I noticed that the compartments for the last three days were still full. Irritated, I marched downstairs, no longer trying to hide my surveillance activities.

"Evan, you haven't been taking your meds," I said through clenched teeth.

He looked up. "I know. I'm not feeling well." He had barely touched his sandwich.

"But that's exactly why you need to take them!" I heard the shrillness in my voice but did not relent. "You have to take your probiotic at least two hours before your midday antibiotic, or else the antibiotic won't work." My heart began pounding, knowing that the Lyme bacteria already had many ways to hide from antibiotics; it didn't need help from Evan.

"And you need the probiotic to build up your immune system so you can eventually get off the antibiotics altogether!" My voice was nearing a full panic.

"I know!" Evan yelled. "Don't you think I want to get better? But I just can't swallow them anymore!"

With his plaintive outburst, my anger began to ebb. I knew that the pills tasted horrible and often made him gag, and the fear of throwing up after downing a handful of pills at one sitting made him increasingly wary of taking his medicine.

I just wanted Even to get better, but that wouldn't happen if he didn't take his medicine. Why couldn't he see that?

"Even Dr. Afrooz says pill fatigue is a real thing," he continued, a hint of defiance in his voice.

My desire to accommodate him immediately evaporated, replaced at lightning speed with a level of annoyance that surprised me. My face flushed with anger, and I turned on my heels and stomped up the stairs. I climbed into bed and pulled the comforter over my head, taking deep breaths through my nose and exhaling through my mouth, willing myself to calm down.

This was my new normal.

Eventually, the dogs barked, signaling that Pete was home from work. I slipped downstairs to the kitchen and began chopping an onion and red peppers for tonight's dinner: homemade pizza.

Pete entered, tossing his jacket on the back of a chair and plopping the bookbag he used in lieu of a briefcase on the floor. He gave me a kiss and asked how my day was. A routine question but not insincere. I updated him on how Evan was feeling, his school progress, and our latest argument.

Pete walked toward me, a sad smile on his face. He wrapped me in his arms, his nose—cold from the winter air—nuzzled my neck as he whispered in my ear, "Thank you for all you're doing." He led me to the couch and motioned for me to sit, then returned to the kitchen to finish making dinner.

The smell of garlic and basil soon filled the air, and like Pavlov's dog, I salivated in anticipation of my favorite comfort food and a glass of red wine.

"Ev, come up and eat!" I called down to Evan in the basement fifteen minutes later.

I wished Evan wasn't up all hours of the night playing video games and chatting with his online "friends." Dr. Afrooz had said it's his way of coping with isolation and the never-ending pain of migraines, which I understood—heck, I enjoyed the dopamine rush I got from winning Candy Crush and solitaire—but it was interfering with his sleep. In fact, he was becoming almost nocturnal, which wreaked havoc on his medicine schedule and his health.

"Evan!" I shouted louder this time. With a huff of annoyance, I trudged down the stairs.

Evan sat in front of the computer, his face brightly illuminated by the reflection of zombies chasing each other. He was wearing headphones, so I raised my arms to get his attention, waving as if stuck on the roadside, flagging down a vehicle. He removed the headphones from one ear and glanced at me as if this was going to be a quick interruption.

"Come up for dinner!" I repeated, the exasperation clear in my voice. Another daily routine.

Evan arrived upstairs annoyed, but I could tell it wasn't aimed at me.

"What's going on?" Pete asked, handing Evan a slice of what passed for pizza these days: dairy-free cheese and vegetables atop a gluten-free cauliflower crust.

"I was playing video games with Tony and Juan, and after our team lost, I texted them with my suggestions for how we could do better in the next game. Tony started telling me how bad I played and how, if it weren't for me, we would have won the game. He said the only reason our team got as many points as we did was because of him."

"Maybe he thought you were criticizing him," I suggested, familiar with the backlash that can come with trying to help someone problem-solve.

"But I wasn't. I even admitted what I thought I could have done better. But then he just told me I suck!"

If only I could still arrange his playdates, he'd stop hanging out with these "friends." But even if he weren't sick, I knew I could no longer control my seventeen-year-old's social activities. I could only hope to steer him in the right direction.

Evan gazed straight head, chewing thoughtfully on his pizza. "What do you guys think is important in a friend?" he asked.

Sensing this wasn't just a philosophical question, I was strategic in my answer. "I think it's someone that you like hanging out with . . . who respects you." And then, "What do you think?"

"Yeah, that, but also someone that you have things in common with," Evan replied. "I don't like Tony so much, but Juan can be cool. We actually have serious conversations about our lives."

I didn't know that. Maybe I needed to stop using air quotes when referring to his online friends.

"But when Juan's with the other guys, they all start making racist and misogynistic jokes. It reminds me of guys in middle school who would ask if I 'tapped that' when I was just talking with a girl."

I bit my tongue and waited, silently imploring Pete to take this one. I was still angry that our current president had recently bragged about grabbing women by the pussy.

"Why do people say things like that? Why do people believe things like that?" Evan continued, clearly distressed.

"I don't know," Pete began. "Maybe it's what they were taught, or maybe they're just saying that stuff because they think it makes them look cool."

Evan shook his head, either in disbelief or in sad recognition of an unfortunate truth.

"Are your high school friends like that?" I asked, purposely pivoting away from his virtual friends.

"No, but I don't see them."

"Emily and Annie stopped by with cookies, and you didn't come to the door," I reminded him. Evan and Emily had been friends since elementary school, and they had just begun dating when he got sick.

"I don't want them to see me like this." Evan gestured to the PICC line peeking out from the orange sock.

"What about your other school friends? Do you keep in touch over social media?" Pete inquired, picking up where I left off.

"Not really. I reached out to a couple guys on Snapchat last fall, and they were like, 'Hey Evan! Where have you been?' I told them I had Lyme disease, but then I didn't hear from them."

A lump formed in my throat, threatening to steal my voice as I struggled to find the right words to say . . . words that would comfort.

"They're just busy, honey. It doesn't mean they don't care," I managed.

"That's just it," Evan said, getting up from the table. "They're busy, and I'm not."

Pete and I watched him place his dirty plate in the sink and descend to the basement. We looked at each other. No words came, but none were necessary. Our tear-rimmed eyes told us all we needed to know about how the other was feeling.

Seeking to lift our spirits, Pete and I typically watched a couple of sitcoms after dinner. Some nights, Evan would join us, and we'd chuckle at the shenanigans taking place on *Brooklyn Nine-Nine* or *black-ish* or *Modern Family*. If we were lucky, we could convince Evan to do an Epsom salt footbath—a treatment recommended by Dr. Afrooz to help remove toxins from his body. Promptly at 9:00 p.m., our shows over, Evan would return to the basement to continue gaming with his friends, and Pete would kiss me good night and head upstairs to bed.

"I'll be up in a bit," I usually said, and I meant it.

Except . . .

The house was so quiet at night that I just wanted to bask in its warm nothingness. No longer on duty—or on edge—my racing thoughts would begin to slow. Most nights, I'd pour a glass of wine and open my gaming apps. At midnight, I'd tune into the late-night shows' opening monologues, amused by the clever political humor, even as I was deeply saddened and often angered by the true stories they referenced. Needing to clear my head, I'd return to my gaming apps, promising myself to play only one more game before going to bed, but inevitably, I would play for another hour or two. With a slight buzz, I'd fall into a fitful sleep around 2:00 a.m.

Chapter 13

February 2017

Evan was now suffering from migraines almost daily, and he also endured bouts of dizziness and nausea and was extremely sensitive to sound. I had hoped that after five months of IV treatments, he'd be feeling better by now. But he wasn't.

I called Dr. Afrooz, begging for something—anything—that might help with his headaches. She suggested a new therapy.

"It's not medicine," she explained. "They're patches that use nanotechnology to provide phototherapy using your body's own heat to reduce inflammation and increase energy. You place the patches at key energy meridians on the body. It's kind of like acupuncture, but instead of needles, you use these patches."

I was skeptical.

"Is there any evidence that they work?"

"There is," she replied. "They've been shown in clinical trials to be effective at reducing cortisol—a stress hormone—and inflammation. Astronauts and athletes use them."

I agreed to start treatment, even as I made a mental note to google the medical research. Knowing that Evan struggled just to get out of bed, and given her office was only five minutes away, Dr. Afrooz offered to come by the house between appointments to begin treatment. I thanked her profusely, my voice quivering with both gratitude and hope.

An hour later, there was a light rap at the front door, which sent our dogs into a frenzy. Evan blurted out an obscenity and jumped up from the sofa where—dressed in the same flannel pajamas he had worn yesterday and the day before that—he had been reclining, his arm slung over his eyes.

"Put Champer and Brady outside, please!" I told Evan sharply as I went to the front door. I was both annoyed and nervous with trepidation, but I suspected that Evan only heard the impatient police officer barking orders. I guided Dr. Afrooz into the family room where Evan now sat, pressing his hands against his temples. He looked up when we entered and smiled weakly at Dr. Afrooz.

I closed the shades as Dr. Afrooz explained to Evan how the treatment worked. She then handed him a bottle of water in which she had added a dropperful of immune-support nutrients and told him to walk around for a minute to circulate those nutrients throughout his system. She then placed a brown patch on Evan's left temple and a white patch on his right temple. Two minutes later, she placed a different patch on the webbed skin between his right thumb and forefinger—the location I learned years earlier that you press to make a headache go away, although it didn't work for Evan's migraines. Dr. Afrooz handed Evan another bottle of nutrient water and instructed him to circle our small family room again.

I watched intently from the corner of the room as if watching a magic trick: wanting to believe but inherently skeptical.

"How is your headache?" Dr. Afrooz asked half an hour later.

"It's almost gone," Evan said, his eyebrows raised in a look of surprise. Then, turning to me, a slow smile creasing his face, "It's almost GONE!"

"On a scale of one to ten, what was it before we started?" I stepped forward, no longer a passive observer of what felt like a miracle.

"An eight or nine," Evan said.

"And now?"

"About a two. It's almost gone!" he repeated . . . but then he paused, a confused look crossing his face. "At least I think it's gone. I've had a headache for so long, I can barely remember what it feels like not to have one."

His comment sliced my heart, devastated that he couldn't remember what it felt like not to be in constant pain. Evan must have seen the stricken look on my face as I fought to stifle my tears, and he walked toward me.

"It's okay, mom." He put his arms around me, and we held each other.

I locked this memory away for the days ahead when I knew I would feel less hopeful.

I didn't have to wait long.

Evan came thumping down the stairs a few days later, laptop in hand, as I sat in my glider rocker, cradling my second cup of coffee of the day.

He poked at his computer screen. "How is that possible?" his voice boomed, his eyebrows knitted in confusion and anger.

I looked where he was pointing and saw that the "percent completed" for each course had gone down since last week. So had his grades.

"I don't know," I replied, dumbstruck. "But I'll find out."

I reached out to the school district's homebound coordinator, but not surprisingly, she was not intimately familiar with how the vendor software calculated the various scores. I played around with the numbers on an Excel spreadsheet and made a startling discovery. The recommended pace of one hour per day per course was more than a goal: It was actually used in the calculation of grades and the calculation of the percent of the course completed. Students who fell behind the recommended-but-really-required pace saw their completion rate and grades drop in direct proportion to how far behind they were. So even though Evan's "overall" grade on his completed history assignments was an eighty-four, because he was completing assignments at half the required rate, his "actual" grade was a forty-two.

"That makes no sense!" Evan had said when I explained it to him, his trembling lower lip conveying both sadness and frustration.

My heart ached. The poor kid just couldn't catch a break. "I know. I'll talk with the homebound coordinator. Meanwhile, please continue working and just ignore those numbers for now."

"But why should I try if I'm not going to get credit for my work?"

"You will. I'll straighten it out. Just keep doing your schoolwork."

"Let them fix it first. Then I'll do my schoolwork," he declared defiantly before snapping the laptop shut and marching back upstairs.

I felt my face flush with anger at his irresponsible attitude, finding yet another excuse not to do his schoolwork. Didn't he realize that his "screw you" stance hurt only him? My face darkened as I recalled a carefully tucked away memory.

My father pulled up to the curb in his tan Ford Falcon, the rusty car door creaking as he opened it and swung it shut. He was here to pick up the six of us kids for our court-mandated weekly visit. I watched through the living room window as he made his way to the front door. Suddenly, my mother burst out the front door and told him to leave, and they began to argue. Just like last week. And the week before. Each week that my father missed or was late in making a child support payment, my mother refused to let him see us kids.

She sued my father for missed child support payments, which required weekly appearances in small claims court. She reveled in going to court each week, snidely commenting to us kids before she left that she was going to stick it to our father. I cringed at those remarks, sowing divisiveness where there was already distance. And why sue my father? It's not like my father was doing well—financially or emotionally. There was a time to fight and a time to move on.

After three years of weekly visits to the Erie County Courthouse, the court decided in my mother's favor. But my father was still unable to pay—"You can't get blood from a stone," he'd often remarked when we did see him—making all her efforts an exercise in futility. Her vindictive spite got her nowhere.

I heard Evan's bedroom door slam shut, and I sighed. Settling back into my gliding rocker, I turned on my laptop. As it slowly hummed to life, I gazed out the window at the desolate February morning, the howling wind choreographing a skeletal dance among the barren trees.

I opened the patient portal to see if the results from Evan's most recent blood work had been posted. They had. I clicked on the PDF file and, taking a deep breath, scanned the column labeled "Flag" for the words High, Low, or Abnormal.

On the first page, this column was blank, indicating normal levels of red and white blood cells, platelets, hemoglobin, and other parts of the blood.

So far, so good.

I scrolled down to the second page, which listed results for various fungal infections. About halfway down the page, I saw a flag indicating that Evan tested positive for *Histoplasma*. Dr. Afrooz had not tested for this previously, so I had no idea what this was. From a quick search of the CDC website, I learned that Histoplasmosis results from breathing in microscopic spores of fungus found in most soils. I knitted my brow in confusion. *When had Evan been near soil recently? Had we tracked infected soil into our home on our sneakers?* I made a mental note to wear slippers inside and wash the floors.

I continued to read. "Although most people who breathe in the spores don't get sick, for some people, such as those who have weakened immune systems, the infection can become severe, especially if it spreads from the lungs to other organs."[8] My heart began to race. I took a steadying breath and continued to read.

The third page showed results from the Comprehensive Metabolic Panel, a routine blood test that measured the amount of important substances in the blood—glucose, calcium, protein, electrolytes—and provided markers of the health of the liver and the kidneys. My eyes were drawn to the bolded word "High" next to the word "creatinine," which I knew was a measure of the amount of impurities in the blood. I stopped cold, knowing full well what it meant. Evan's kidney functioning was compromised. Icy fingers gripped my heart.

I kept scrolling as if playing with a jack-in-the-box, certain that something scary was going to jump out at me but feeling compelled to continue, nonetheless.

The fourth page contained results from the Lyme Western blot, which Dr. Afrooz reran to see if there had been any change since Evan's original diagnosis of "possibly clinically significant" nine months ago. There hadn't. Evan continued to test positive. *Wasn't the IV medicine making any difference?* With sagging shoulders and a heavy sigh, I continued to scroll. And that's when I saw it.

For the first time, Evan tested positive for Rocky Mountain spotted fever. Unlike most of the bacteria and fungi tested, I had heard of Rocky Mountain spotted fever, or RMSF, but I didn't know how serious it was.

I opened a new tab and typed in "Rocky Mountain spotted fever." From the Harvard Medical School's website, I learned that Rocky Mountain spotted fever was a severe illness in which the *Rickettsia rickettsii* bacteria damaged the linings of blood vessels and could cause serious bleeding, kidney damage, and even kidney failure. The icy fingers now poked at my heart as if taunting me. "Treatment with doxycycline is critical to survival,"[9] screamed the CDC website in bold font.

The fact that Evan had already been treated with doxycycline did little to assuage my growing fears. Until now, the thought that Evan could die from his illness had never crossed my mind.

I'd always been good in a crisis. Rather than panic, crises always seemed to hone my ability to problem-solve with crystal-clear focus—like the day my mother helped me move to Washington, DC, after college to start my job at the US Department of Health and Human Services.

She had been humming softly as we sped down the highway in her rusty, two-toned green Ford Granada, towing a small U-Haul containing my meager belongings. Brian was in the back seat doing his "work"—copying words out of an old *TV Guide* magazine into a notebook—giggling to himself. Abruptly, Brian's giggles stopped.

"Ohh . . . Ohhh! OHHH!" he had moaned with increasing intensity.

I looked back and saw him squirming in his seat.

"Mom! Pull over! Brian's seat is smoking!" We later learned that the catalytic converter had overheated and burned through the heat shield, igniting the back seat cushion.

Frantic, my mother had yanked the steering wheel sharply to the right to pull over, and we began to fishtail.

"What-do-I-do? What-do-I-do?" my mother cried. We were on a bridge stretching a half-mile ahead over a marsh far below, and we were heading for the guardrail.

"Just ease up on the gas," I had calmly directed her as if I had done this before. "Now hold the wheel firmly and don't overcompensate. Slowly steer back into the lane."

Safely across the bridge, my mother pulled the car to a stop on the right shoulder. Crisis averted.

Ice in my veins, they call it. I call it a refusal to give in to fear, panic, and despair.

But now? I felt my stubborn optimism begin to crack as if I had stepped onto a frozen lake, realizing too late that it couldn't hold my weight as I began to sink into its cold, murky depths.

Chapter 14

March 2017

I sat in the small waiting room, fidgeting slightly as I surveyed the familiar surroundings of my nephrologist's office. Four chairs and one loveseat, all of which were empty except for the padded wooden chair in which I sat. The three paintings on the wall together formed a single landscape of a meadow dotted with wildflowers in muted shades of pink and purple. The 3D models of kidneys sat adorning the windowsill. Even with my all-encompassing focus on Evan's health, I was mindful not to neglect my own—especially given my family history of kidney disease.

Not only did my mother die from end-stage renal failure, but so did her mother and three of her five siblings. Each had a different type of kidney disease, and none were genetic, the family narrative went. This was so rare that their nephrologist wanted to share this medical mystery in the premier medical publication *The Journal of the American Medical Association*. I don't know if he ever did, nor do I know how much of this family lore was true, but I wasn't going to take any chances.

Soon after Pete and I had married and moved to Virginia, I sought out a nephrologist. At my first appointment nearly twenty-five years ago, Dr. Assefi had ordered a sonogram and blood work to get a baseline of my kidney functioning. The sonogram revealed a single kidney.

I was astonished. Nothing in my family history had prepared me for that curveball.

Dr. Assefi had said that I probably had a kidney infection as a toddler that had damaged my left kidney and that it had been atrophying ever since. The remaining kidney was functioning at sixty percent capacity— reflecting diminished but sufficient kidney functioning—so Dr. Assefi wasn't worried. In fact, with only one kidney, he said he'd expected a number closer to fifty percent—half capacity—so my single working kidney was doing a great job clearing impurities from my body.

"What about having children?" I had asked at that first appointment. Dr. Assefi confirmed that while pregnancy does take a toll on the mother's kidneys, my kidney functioning was sufficient to withstand pregnancy.

Within a year, I was pregnant with Matthew, my "gift from God." Both Dr. Assefi and my OB-GYN monitored my kidney functioning closely. When my creatinine rose steeply during the last four weeks of my pregnancy, signaling a buildup of impurities in my body, my OB-GYN had declared: "Let's give this baby an eviction notice!" Labor was induced, and Matthew was born five days early, completely healthy.

By the time I became pregnant with Evan two years later, my kidney functioning had dipped a bit but was holding steady. But once again, during my last month of pregnancy, my creatinine rose quickly, requiring that Evan also be induced. He was born almost three weeks early, healthy as his brother at birth and even a few ounces heavier. Noticing the trend, I asked Dr. Assefi and my OB-GYN whether a third pregnancy might require an even earlier—dangerously early—delivery due to stress on my kidneys. They said it was likely. So, Pete and I had agreed: Our family was complete with Matthew and Evan.

Today's appointment with Dr. Assefi was my semiannual checkup. The nurse-doubling-as-a-receptionist led me to the examination room, where she took my blood pressure.

"One-ten over seventy-four," she said. "Very good!"

High blood pressure was very common in chronic kidney disease, so I took comfort in every blood pressure reading that was normal—which had been all of them so far.

"Dr. Assefi will be right in." She smiled warmly as she turned to leave, closing the door behind her.

"Hallo, Sharon!" he sang out in accented English. Tall and elegant, his hair much grayer than when I had first met him, Dr. Assefi extended his hand, enfolding mine in a handshake that was both professional and comforting. "How are you feeling, dear?"

"A little tired." Fatigue was a symptom of worsening kidney disease, given the extra effort required for the kidneys to eliminate toxins and impurities from the blood. "But other than that, I feel fine."

He consulted his clipboard containing the results from my recent tests. "Let's see here . . . your kidney functioning is twenty-nine percent," he said matter-of-factly.

Having already reviewed these results in the patient portal, my heart nevertheless clenched at the stark reality: This was the first time my kidney functioning had dropped below thirty percent, signaling Stage 4 of chronic kidney disease. Stage 5, when the kidneys were operating at less than fifteen percent capacity, indicated end-stage renal failure, at which time I would need dialysis or a kidney transplant.

"When can I get on the list?" I leaned forward in earnest.

When my mother was diagnosed with end-stage renal disease in 1985, she didn't want to be placed on the kidney transplant list. She said she wasn't ready—which I never understood. When it's a matter of life and death, don't you find a way to get ready? To do what you're supposed to? I would not make that same mistake.

"When your kidney functioning drops below twenty percent," Dr. Assefi replied, "I will recommend that you begin the kidney transplant evaluation process. Unless the doctors discover a serious disease or an untreatable health condition, they will place you on the transplant list. At that time, you can begin reaching out to friends and family to see if they'd like to get tested to be a live donor."

Kidneys from live donors were preferred to those from deceased donors, I knew, because they tended to last longer and were less likely to be rejected by the recipient's immune system.

I sat processing the onslaught of information, looking not so much at Dr. Assefi but through him, trying to picture my future.

"I want you to attend this class"—he handed me a brochure—"which explains more about chronic kidney disease, a kidney-friendly diet, and options for dialysis."

Dialysis.

An image of my mother filled my mind: the catheter attached to her abdomen, connected to the bag of saline solution hanging from an IV pole. The liquid filled her peritoneal cavity, absorbing impurities and excess fluids until, four hours later, she'd drain the waste-filled peritoneal fluid into a separate bag, completing one of six arduous but life-saving kidney dialysis exchanges she did each day.

"And the next time I see you," Dr. Assefi's baritone voice startled me back to the present, "I want to see a water bottle in there." He gestured to my oversized purse, his eyebrows raised, gently chastising me. "You should be drinking lots of water throughout the day."

With a handshake and a slight bow, he said goodbye, instructing me to make an appointment for three months from now—the increased frequency not lost on me—which I did. If I learned anything from my childhood, it was that failing to take care of your health could have disastrous consequences.

Chapter 15

May 2017

Evan tapped his foot to the Top 40 song playing on the radio as we backed out of the driveway. His sunglasses and unkempt beard made him look like a bad-boy movie star.

"Oh, wow," Evan murmured, his mouth hanging open in awe. He pointed to the azaleas bursting with red and pink blooms dotting our neighbors' yards.

A wave of admiration swept over me as if seeing my teenage son for the first time. Here he was, struggling with a chronic illness that robbed him of so much, yet he could still see beauty in the world.

Ten minutes later, we pulled up to the two-story brick building housing Dr. Afrooz's office. As usual, I had reviewed Evan's test results before our appointment. Evan continued to test positive for Lyme disease and for Rocky Mountain spotted fever. In fact, his RMSF titer was 1:128 compared to 1:64 in January. I wasn't sure, but that didn't sound like an improvement. I needed to clarify with Dr. Afrooz.

For the first time, Evan's blood also showed slightly elevated levels of urea nitrogen, a waste product removed by the kidneys. I told myself that it was likely the bacterial, viral, and antifungal die-off from all the medicine Evan was taking and that the higher numbers were to be expected. I didn't dare consider the alternative—that his kidneys were failing.

At least Evan was done with his IV treatments, I thought optimistically. Evan had never been so happy about his weekly nurse visit. "Now, some people get a little woozy," the nurse had said as she readied our dining room table to remove Evan's PICC line. Rather than feeling impersonal, her matter-of-fact tone conveyed a sense of competence that was comforting and elicited trust. With gloved hands, she had gently peeled away the tape holding Evan's PICC line in place and slowly pulled the PICC line out of his arm. I had watched as Evan's expression turned from calm to unease to wonderment.

"So weird!" he'd said. "I can feel it coming out, starting way over here." He pointed to just above his heart. My knees still weakened at the memory.

We were hopeful that the end of Evan's IV treatment meant that he was cured, but as we pulled into the parking lot and made our way up the flight of stairs to Dr. Afrooz's office, I prepared myself for bad news. Despite my best efforts to exorcise this childhood habit of expecting the worst, it clung stubbornly to the deepest parts of me, like an unseen pathogen that remained dormant until it reemerged opportunistically to feed on my fears.

"How are you feeling?" Dr. Afrooz asked Evan as we settled ourselves in her office.

"My concentration is a little better, and I have more energy," Evan began, "but I'm still tired most of the time. And I still get headaches, but they're not as bad."

Evan's headaches were now less frequent and less severe, which had greatly improved his mood and energy, allowing him to tackle his schoolwork on a more regular basis. He had even made it to a chaperoned sleepover with his posse of friends last month. It didn't matter that he called me before midnight asking to be picked up; he had spent a few hours out of the house with his real friends.

"Hmm. Most of my patients are better after IV treatment." Dr. Afrooz tappity-tapped on the computer keyboard, bringing up Evan's latest blood work results.

"Unfortunately"—she turned to Evan—"you still tested positive for Rocky Mountain spotted fever. That would explain your continued headaches and fatigue."

"What does it mean that his titer is now 1:128 when it was 1:64 three months ago?"

Dr. Afrooz explained that the second number referred to the number of antibodies in the blood sample: An increase in that number was evidence of a recent or ongoing infection. But she told me not to worry. As she had explained back in January, Evan's antibiotic treatments for Lyme disease were also addressing his Rocky Mountain spotted fever infection. She was also not concerned about the elevated urea nitrogen in Evan's blood.

"It's only slightly elevated," she noted. "He may just be dehydrated."

I made a mental note to keep pushing liquids on Evan and to have Dr. Afrooz check this again in next month's blood work.

She swiveled away from her computer and looked at me. "Have you checked your house for mold?"

Dr. Afrooz had recommended this last fall, but with everything going on, I had only gotten around to it in March.

"Yes, a couple months ago." I pulled out a manilla folder containing the mold test results. "We had an industrial hygienist test our home, and he found surface mold in the basement on the exposed wood beams in the laundry room, in the closet under the stairs, and in the small room we used for storage. But thankfully, there was no evidence of airborne mold spores." I knew from my research that airborne spores could wreak havoc on Evan's respiratory system.

That two-hour visit by the industrial hygienist and the testing for mold had cost us $1,200. We decided against hiring a professional to clean the visible mold—some wanted as much as $10,000 to thoroughly sanitize and deodorize the basement. Instead, we purchased the recommended chemical, rented a pesticide respirator from Lowes, and did the work ourselves. Pete and I scrubbed the visible growth and fumigated the basement to remediate any remaining mold. We threw out anything that could support the growth of mold, including the fabric sofa, wall-to-wall carpeting, and all kinds of memorabilia.

That last action had left me heartbroken. Standing in the doorway, my eyes swept the musty storage room full of trifold science fair projects tucked away in a corner, saltwater maps of Virginia stacked neatly high upon a shelf, and boxes safely protecting memories of childhood milestones: mobiles from the boys' cribs, artwork from preschool, the laminated nametags the boys had worn on their first day of kindergarten, Scooby-Doo and Batman lunch boxes. Gently placed on top of the boxes lay signs from the lemonade stands that Evan had held over the years, a child's handwriting exclaiming, "It's sweltering outside!" and "Ahh . . . It's refreshing!"

I had carried the science fair projects, the saltwater maps, the boxes of treasures, and the lemonade stand signs up the basement stairs and into the garage. With the recycling bin to my left and the garbage can to my right, I had cradled each item in my hand—sometimes holding it to my heart—smiling at the memories it elicited. I snapped a picture, sometimes two, of each item with my phone, then placed the item in the proper bin, my heart twisting with sadness. Before the grief became overwhelming, I had reminded myself that I was doing what I needed to do—what was best for Evan—even if that meant letting go of the past in order to move forward. With that thought, I had finished the task with workmanlike efficiency.

Dr. Afrooz listened intently, nodding her head, but her face remained quizzical.

She prescribed vitamin B12 shots (oh God, not more needles!), ordered lab work, and asked to see him again in one month.

On the drive home, Evan expressed his frustration. "I just hate getting my hopes up," he lamented, his body slumped in the front seat, no longer interested in the world coming to life around him. "It's almost better to assume I won't ever get better."

His comment saddened me, but I was surprised by another, stronger emotion: panic. Panic that he would become despondent and give up.

I found my mother sobbing at our kitchen table, her body heaving with despair, a near-empty bottle of wine within arm's reach. My body began to quake with a sense of dread as my fifteen-year-old self slowly moved toward her, stammering, "Wh—what's wrong?"

She looked up at me with red-rimmed eyes, her vacant expression scaring me more than her slurred speech. "I miss my parents."

Her mother had recently died at the age of sixty-six after a failed kidney transplant, and her father had died from a heart attack five years earlier at the age of sixty—a shock to the family not only because of his young age but also because he had received a clean bill of health from his physician only weeks earlier, which had permanently soured my mother on going to the doctor.

"I've lived my life. I'm so tired," she heaved.

She was forty.

I stared at my mother, her once indomitable spirit crushed under the weight of life's misfortunes. It was then that I realized she was not just sad; she was deeply depressed and depleted of hope. Frozen in place, not knowing how to help her, I felt utterly useless. How did you break free from depression when depression itself robbed you of any motivation to seek help? A cruel catch-22. My mother was stuck, and there was nothing I could do or say to get her unstuck.

Chapter 16

June 2017

Evan's goal was to graduate high school on time, one year from now, which would require that he complete eleventh grade before school started at the end of August. He completed his history course in late May, and we had celebrated with a fondue dinner at The Melting Pot, resurrecting an end-of-school-year tradition from before Evan had gotten sick. That left only English for him to finish up over the summer.

Sympathetic to our dilemma regarding the educational software's pacing guide, Evan's principal, Dr. Brewer, and Mrs. Amodeo agreed to a new set of benchmarks that did not eliminate the pacing penalty but lessened its impacts on Evan's course completion rate and grades. Evan and I took it as a win.

Coupled with getting a handle on his sleep schedule with the help of melatonin, Evan began doing homework on a regular basis. He had even established a routine for himself: He'd set a goal for how many assignments he'd complete on a given day and, if he felt up to it, he'd complete additional assignments until his fatigue or foggy brain got the best of him. He was also eating more frequently, microwaving frozen sausage-and-egg sandwiches for breakfast and noshing on dinner leftovers at all times of the day and night.

With this progress, Pete and I felt comfortable joining his sisters and their families for our annual beach trip to Dewey Beach, Delaware. Preferring a quiet house to himself where he could focus on schoolwork, Evan decided to pass again this year. I, on the other hand, was looking forward to this trip, having missed it last summer to stay at home with Evan.

I let Evan know that I would continue to monitor his progress while we were away. Thank goodness I had requested access to his online dashboard when he was still a minor; he could legally remove my access to his account this fall when he turned eighteen. I decided not to tell him he would soon have that right.

I am not a helicopter parent, I reassured myself as we crossed the Chesapeake Bay Bridge, the sun glittering on the rippled water far below. I knew that it was developmentally appropriate, necessary even, for adolescents to have increasing autonomy to make their own decisions and learn firsthand the consequences of those decisions. But I also knew—as a researcher and from personal experience—that some decisions had lasting consequences that could not be undone.

No, I decided, this was a time to be more engaged, more vigilant . . . not less.

We arrived at our beachfront motel, quickly unloaded the car, changed into our bathing suits, and joined our family already rollicking on the beach.

I watched Pete and Matthew chase our nephews in the sand, the boys' giggles mingling with the caw of seagulls flying overhead. The boys' frivolity felt distant, two-dimensional, as if I were watching this scene on TV.

Sitting with my sisters-in-law at the shore's edge, paperbacks splayed open on our laps unread and our feet nestled in the wet sand, we chatted about everything and nothing. I turned my face toward the sun, begging for its warm embrace, but I felt only its hot sting.

"I'm so glad you guys are here, but I'm sorry Evan didn't feel up to coming." Alyssa's ever-present effervescent smile dimmed with sadness.

Instinctively, I wanted to ease her concerns with a positive spin—"His health is on the upswing, we think" and "At least he's making good progress on his homework"—but the words died in my throat.

"Yeah, me too," I murmured.

Even without Alyssa's reminder, I thought of Evan constantly. This was the longest I had been away from him since his diagnosis, and it felt strange, as if an unseen umbilical cord had been cut, and now, untethered, I floated aimlessly with no direction and no purpose. I hadn't felt this helpless since I was a child.

Hours later, with the sun setting and our pink faces reminding us to reapply sunscreen the following day, I sat on the deck of the condo where my sister-in-law and her family were staying, sipping a cold beer. I could hear my nephew's muffled squeals of delight coming from inside, and, turning to the window, I saw Pete licking whipped cream off his face, having lost the most recent round of Pie Face. I was glad he was having fun. Although he's not one to volunteer how he's feeling, I knew Pete was every bit as concerned about Evan as I was. He just had an easier time relaxing and trusting that Evan was doing what he needed to and that things would work out.

I, on the other hand, was preoccupied with how Evan was faring with his English course. His Lyme-addled brain caused him to struggle with reading comprehension and writing coherent essays, which frustrated him and often resulted in his putting off assignments until he felt better. He had been a voracious reader and a good writer before Lyme disease, and it pained me to witness these tiny deaths. I took a swig of beer and looked up at the powder-blue sky dusted with high clouds, gathering my thoughts about the phone call I had received an hour ago.

Evan's English teacher had expressed her concern about how far behind Evan was. She informed me that if Evan didn't finish English 11 by the mid-August deadline six weeks from now, he wouldn't have time to finish high school before he turned nineteen—the age at which students aged out of high school in our district—and he would have to obtain his GED instead. The deadline for making this decision was this Friday.

I shared the conversation with Pete, who felt confident that Evan could finish on time. I wasn't so sure. Unlike Pete, I knew how many assignments Evan had left and how long it was taking him to complete those assignments, and the math just didn't add up. At the same time, I wanted Evan to know that we believed in him. Was this the time to be optimistic or realistic?

Pete appeared at the door and told me that dinner was ready. The smell of garlic and the sounds of laughter wafted out the door and drew me inside, where a plate of lasagna and a glass of red wine awaited me.

Hours later, with our nephews safely tucked into bed and the kitchen cleaned, Pete, Matthew, and I hugged our family goodbye and walked back to our motel a half mile away. I breathed the humid night air. The sea breeze, warm on my skin, nevertheless caused my skin to prickle. Arriving back at the motel, I said good night to Matthew, then drafted a text to Evan—he was more likely to respond by text than answer his phone—and hit Send.

Tuesday, June 27, 2017

> Mom: Your English teacher called to say she is concerned about how far behind you are. She has some ideas to help you catch up. I am confident you can complete English by the August 11 deadline, but it will require a HUGE commitment on your part to work many hours EVERY day. *Please let me know before Friday.* Dad, Matthew, and I are here to help however we can. Love, Mom. 10:11 PM

I checked my texts for the next thirty minutes, and when Evan didn't respond, I turned off the lights and went to sleep.

The stream of morning sunlight through the partially drawn curtains woke me up, and the promise of free coffee and donuts in the motel lobby drew me out of bed. There was no sign of Pete or the dogs; he must have taken them for a walk, I surmised.

Remembering last night, I grabbed my cell phone. Nothing from Evan, but there was an email from the director of homebound instruction requesting that we chat by phone. Like me, she had reservations about Evan's ability to complete the remainder of his English course in the next six weeks. We scheduled a call for early afternoon.

When Pete returned with the dogs ten minutes later then, I showed him the email. Pete still believed that Evan could do it, but he was open to talking with the director of homebound instruction to get her thoughts and discuss options.

I texted Evan after the call.

Wednesday, June 28, 2017

> Mom: Dad and I just talked to the director of homebound instruction. We think it would be best if you dropped English 11. Let's chat . . . give me a call. 1:10 PM

I had barely put down my phone when it buzzed.

> Evan: No. Have some friggin faith in me. English will be done by August. Trust me or don't. I don't care anymore. I have been getting so much work done by basically ignoring both of you. When you get home do not say a word to me about school. 1:17 PM

Whoa. I did not expect that reaction. My initial inclination was to reply with: "Don't talk to me like that!" But I liked the spunk he showed. He clearly cared about finishing by August and was committed to doing so. This was the most motivated I'd seen him since he became ill, and relief washed over me, buoying my spirits.

I showed the text to Pete, who chuckled and said simply, "All right, then!"

> Mom: I'm so sorry to upset you. Dad and I absolutely trust you. We were trying to make it more manageable for you. 1:27 PM

With newfound confidence in Evan, Pete and I said nothing to Evan about schoolwork when we returned home from the beach.

Chapter 17

August 2017

Evan finished English 11 by the August deadline with a passing grade and was promoted to his senior year. Now we just had to figure out how he would undertake twelfth grade.

Like last year, Pete and I hoped that Evan would be able to go to school in person. But unlike last year, we now had a better sense of Evan's illness and what he could manage. Not surprisingly, Evan was hesitant to commit to taking his classes in person, even though he was beginning to feel better and needed only four courses to graduate. I continued to believe that Evan wouldn't know what he was capable of until he tried. "Shoot for the moon, and if you miss, you'll still land among the stars." Isn't that how the saying went?

Pete and I suggested that Evan attend his high school's "Zero Day"—a three-hour block of time set aside the week before classes started to have students attend their classes in fifteen-minute blocks to meet their teachers, obtain their syllabi, and learn about course expectations. Still skeptical, Evan grudgingly agreed.

Dr. Afrooz had recommended that Evan begin physical therapy to increase his muscle tone and stamina, but he had refused, despite my encouragement and reassurance that he could cancel any appointment he didn't feel up to attending. So, to prepare Evan for his return to school, Pete suggested that Evan join him on his evening walks with our dogs to help him build up his stamina after being virtually bedbound for nearly six months. Pete worked out every morning and was a strong believer in the healing power of exercise. Some days, Evan could do it, and he returned home beaming at his ability to walk the five minutes to school and back, albeit tired from the exertion. Other days, however, Evan barely had the energy to get out of bed.

Zero Day arrived, and we decided to drive the quarter mile to school so Evan could save his energy for navigating the halls to his classes. The crush of students and parents entering the building had me worried; Evan hadn't been around this many people in almost eighteen months, and my hands began to sweat just thinking about how overwhelmed he must have felt. I looked at my nervous child, his prairie dog eyes darting left and right with a wariness that caused my heart to ache. Still, he moved forward through the crowd.

We followed Evan to his classrooms, trailing behind a respectable distance as he nodded hello to acquaintances and returned boisterous high fives from friends on the basketball team, one of whom yelled over the din, "Hey, Evan! Where have you been? We thought you were dead!" I cringed at the comment, and I looked over at Pete, who was chuckling.

"Kids," he muttered with a shrug and a playful roll of his eyes.

I began to relax. Maybe this would work?

Driving home three hours later, I asked Evan how he was feeling.

"Terrible." Slumped in the back seat of the car, he looked like a leaky balloon, slowly deflating. "My head is killing me, my joints hurt, and I'm exhausted. There's no way I can go to school in person."

I was proud of him for trying—I really was. So why was my jaw clenched with irritation?

Chapter 18

September 2017

With dark circles under his eyes and a scowl on his face, Evan looked especially tired and grumpy when he entered the kitchen that morning. He grabbed a Jimmy Dean egg sandwich from the freezer, ripped it from its plastic wrapper, tossed it into the microwave, slammed the door shut with a bang, and punched the keyboard with his index finger as if poking an enemy in the chest.

"Everything okay?" I ventured cautiously. *Do I really want to know?* my inner voice whispered, not in the mood to listen to his complaints. Shocked at my lack of sympathy, I turned toward Evan and offered a smile that I hoped looked sincere.

Evan's face softened slightly, suggesting annoyance more than anger. "When I have a headache or can't concentrate, I just want to knock off a lesson or two and save the quizzes and tests for when I feel better."

Not unreasonable, and yet I can't help feeling that he's making excuses for not tackling the more difficult work.

"But the software makes me complete activities in order—first the lessons, then the quizzes, then the tests—before moving on to the next module."

"Is that why you haven't logged in for the past couple of days?"

Evan nodded, his shoulders slumped in defeat.

It pained me to watch Evan fall further and further behind and get increasingly discouraged as a result. A vicious cycle. Images of Evan spiraling downward and falling into a pit of despair filled my mind.

"You said you were feeling okay the other day—why didn't you try the test then?" I was aiming for encouragement, but even *I* heard the accusation in my voice.

Pete entered the room, probably sensing a brewing argument that he anticipated having to mediate. Again.

"Because I was working on another class!" Evan growled.

"But your grades and completion rates get worse if you don't work on each class for at least an hour every day!" I should know by now that pushing Evan beyond his capabilities didn't work, but I couldn't seem to stop myself. The thought of him giving up terrified me.

The call came as I was getting ready for bed. It was late 1989, and I was a 25-year-old still trying to find my footing in my first job in a new city.

"Sharon?" his voice croaked.

My father was calling from Florida, where he had lived since 1979 with his second wife. I later learned they had divorced only months before this call.

My heart raced. My father only called with bad news.

He explained that he had lost his job and didn't know what to do. I had no idea where my father worked or why he lost his job, and I didn't ask. I assumed he was still in sales, and I assumed he was fired for his drinking. I thought that he might qualify for unemployment benefits and food stamps while he looked for another job. I told him this and promised to look into how to access those services in his community.

"Meanwhile, I can send you some money."

Unlike previous calls, my father did not sound relieved. His cracked voice whispered, "Thank you," but it sounded more like "Goodbye." His sense of hopelessness was palpable, even over the phone. I was frantic. There had to be something more I could do! There was always a solution, wasn't there? I just needed to find it.

But nothing seemed to matter to him anymore. I felt time slipping away, my constant worry about my father growing into full-blown panic.

Six months later, my mother called to tell me that my father had died. He was found in his decrepit Florida home—more shanty than house—with no food in the refrigerator and bags of empty vodka bottles scattered throughout the living room. Among his meager belongings was an old Polaroid of us six kids tucked away in a rusty metal box. He was fifty-four years old, and he died utterly alone.

"Can't you just do SOMETHING?" I implored, frustration morphing into panic.

"Mom! Just stop!"

"I'm just saying! I don't want you to fall so far behind that you give up."

"Would you just SHUT THE HELL UP?" Evan screamed, his eyes boring into mine with an intensity I had never seen before.

"Don't talk to me that way!" I shot back, tired of being at the receiving end of his uncharacteristic tirades. I turned to Pete for backup. "Are you going to let him talk to me like that?"

"I get how he's feeling," Pete said simply. In front of Evan. Two against one.

"Are you fucking kidding me?" I screeched at Pete, incredulous.

I felt betrayed by the one person I thought always had my back. I was tired of Pete's laissez-faire parenting that not only made me look like the bad guy but also undermined any effort I made to establish expectations for Evan and be clear on what was and was not acceptable behavior.

A deep chill wracked my body as it often did during interpersonal conflict, flexing muscle memories from childhood. Like an enraged caged animal, I felt a desperate need to escape. I grabbed my purse and stormed out of the house. Jumping into my car, I drove away, not sure where I was going but crystal clear on what I was leaving behind.

I drove west, toward the Blue Ridge Mountains and Virginia's wine country. At a red light, I searched the web for a nearby winery and set my GPS.

I arrived at the winery, grabbed an outside table in the sun, and immediately began to calm, taking in the mountain views with a glass of crisp, cold sauvignon blanc.

I replayed the argument with Evan and Pete in my head. With the perspective that only time and space could provide—aided by a glass of wine—I realized that the sicker Evan became, the more I seemed to push him, as if by stubborn persistence alone, we could outsmart this illness. In fact, any time Evan faced an obstacle, my instinct was to double down on his being responsible. But why? I knew he had a debilitating illness, and I empathized with his situation—I really did!

I closed my eyes, turned my face toward the sun, and considered the question: Why did I feel the need to push Evan so hard?

Tired of thinking, I debated grabbing another glass of wine. I wasn't ready to go home, but neither did I want to spend the day at this winery; I'd already been here over an hour. Then, an idea hit me, and I texted Matthew.

Saturday, September 23, 2017

> Mom: Would you like company this weekend? I feel the need for a mini get-away. 11:11 AM

I smiled at the speed with which he responded and the exclamation point punctuating his response of "Sure!" If Matthew detected any concern, he didn't show it.

I texted Pete, letting him know that I would be at Virginia Tech with Matthew for the weekend. He replied simply, "Have fun." I knew his comment was sincere, not sarcastic, for which I was grateful. But I was still angry with him.

I booked a one-night stay at a hotel in downtown Blacksburg, exited the winery parking lot, then set off down Interstate 81-S, stopping only once to pick up a T-shirt and some underwear at Target. On the road again, I felt my breath slow as I took in the autumn-colored Blue Ridge Mountains to my left and the equally glorious Allegheny Mountains to my right.

I arrived by mid-afternoon. Matthew and I decided to walk the Huckleberry Trail whose trailhead began two blocks from my hotel and meandered through Blacksburg neighborhoods to Lane Stadium and beyond. It was a perfect fall day—warm on the sunny patches of asphalt but cool in the shade of the huckleberry bushes, the occasional breeze producing goosebumps that quickly melted away in the next sunny patch.

Matthew and I walked in companionable silence as I chewed on my hoodie's drawstring, trying to decide what to tell him about my argument with Pete and Evan. I didn't want to leave him in the dark, like I had with Evan's illness last winter, and I certainly didn't want to pretend that everything was fine, like my family did when I was growing up. So I told Matthew the whole story.

"Evan yelled at me to 'shut the hell up,' and Dad didn't stick up for me." I felt my pulse quicken as I retold the story.

Matthew was quiet for a moment, and I knew that my still-waters-run-deep child was thinking about how best to respond.

"Evan was probably just mad at the situation, not you," Matthew suggested, his tone gentle.

A wise insight, but that didn't make me feel any better. "I still think there should be boundaries," I countered, my voice tremulous but firm.

Unsure whether it was the chill in the air or the involuntary shudder of facing conflict, my skin prickled, and I was grateful for the burst of sunlight and warmth that greeted us on the next stretch of path.

"I get it. You're trying so hard to help Evan, and him yelling at you makes you feel unappreciated."

I smiled inwardly at my emotionally intelligent child. My tight shoulders began to relax, and my anger at Pete and Evan slowly began to ebb. The breeze had picked up, and the sweet smell of huckleberry wafted across the trail. I inhaled deeply, then turned to Matthew. "But enough about me. How are you doing, sweetie?"

Matthew filled me in on his classes and how things were going with his girlfriend. He told me that he was considering changing majors. He shared both joys and stresses, and I basked in the wonderful normality of it all.

The sun was low in the western sky, and a chill persisted even in the sunbathed portions of the trail, convincing us to turn around and head back to my hotel. We hugged goodbye for the evening—Matthew had a date with his girlfriend—and agreed to meet up for breakfast the next morning, after which I drove home.

Arriving home, I approached the front door with trepidation, my feet leaden with every step. I tucked a strand of wayward hair behind my ears, took a deep breath, and crossed the threshold.

Evan greeted me at the door and immediately apologized for his outburst, enveloping me in a tight hug. My heart calmed, and I was filled with gratitude that Pete and I had taught our boys about healthy conflict resolution.

"I forgive you," I said, then gently pulled away and clasped his shoulders, looking him square in the eye. "Don't EVER talk to me that way again." He nodded sheepishly, then ascended the stairs to his room.

I turned to Pete, who had watched that exchange and now stood next to me. He gave me a light kiss on the lips, and we embraced.

"Can we talk?" I asked, then led Pete down the hall to the family room, where we took a seat next to each other on the couch.

"I wasn't taking Evan's side," Pete began, anticipating my concern. "I understand where you're coming from, and I understand where he's coming from. He's frustrated, and he lashed out."

"I know he's frustrated. But that doesn't give him the right to treat me disrespectfully," I countered.

I scanned Pete's face for a reaction. Did I detect a small nod?

"It also doesn't mean we shouldn't have any expectations of him," I continued. "For example, I think he should bring up his own dirty dishes from the basement, but you're constantly cleaning up after him!"

I felt my body begin to quake, and I paused, reminding myself that Pete and I were a team. He was not the enemy—the damned Lyme disease was. I started over.

"Look, I know that serving others is your love language, and I appreciate that. But when you do everything for him, he doesn't learn about being responsible. Sometimes, you need to back off and let him take responsibility for doing what he needs to do."

"I agree. I think that applies to his meds and school too."

Wait, what? Did he just use my argument against me? I did not relent. "The stakes are higher if he doesn't take his meds or do his schoolwork," I pointed out, arms crossed defiantly across my chest.

"But pushing him doesn't make him do it." Pete's voice was not argumentative but soft, like when he'd read bedtime stories to the boys.

"Sometimes it does," I replied quietly, not ready to concede his point.

But he was right. The stark reality was that I couldn't make Evan take his medicine, or do his homework, or see his real friends, and pushing him to be responsible and persevere only left him feeling judged, misunderstood, and not supported.

I needed to find a way to motivate Evan and keep him moving forward without pushing him.

Chapter 19

October 2017

Last night, we celebrated Evan's eighteenth birthday.
We didn't invite family over, nor did I buy a cake or ice cream: sugar, dairy, and gluten were inflammatory and only aggravated Evan's symptoms. Still, Evan seemed to enjoy the cauliflower-crust pizza from his favorite restaurant—the homemade mozzarella cheese a treat and a temporary hiatus from his dairy-free diet—and streaming the latest *Spiderman* movie with Pete and me.

It wasn't how I envisioned commemorating this milestone. I had pictured a big family gathering with banners and balloons announcing "Look Who's 18?" and "Time to Adult!" I envisioned his friends—his "real" friends—picking him up in a parent's car to carouse around the shops and restaurants at the local town center, with me calling after him to "have fun, be safe!"

I mourned the end of Evan's childhood . . . and not just the typical nostalgia about lemonade stands and lunch boxes. I mourned the abrupt end of basketball games and band concerts, the untimely end to Evan's dating, the unforeseen end to in-person school attendance, and the virtual evaporation of my teenage son's social life.

At the same time, I dreaded Evan's new legal status as an adult. Evan could now decide to stop all medical treatment or drop out of school, and there was nothing Pete nor I could do, legally, to stop him. Thankfully, we had a close relationship with our boys; they knew we had their best interests at heart, and they valued our advice. Besides, I reminded myself, Evan didn't have the wherewithal to manage communications and appointments with Dr. Afrooz and Mrs. Amodeo—the invisible but critical work of caregiving—even if he wanted to.

Sipping my morning coffee in my glider rocker, I watched a pair of frisky squirrels scamper along the top of our narrow wooden fence, somehow managing to keep their balance. The late morning sun shining through the trees turned the autumn leaves into a kaleidoscope of reds, yellows, and oranges. Since quitting my job almost a year ago, I had come to treasure these quiet mornings, no longer waking with thoughts of to-do lists and a sense of urgency that used to dominate my morning routine.

Despite last night's muted but pleasant celebration, Evan woke in a sour mood, a scowl plastered on his face as he entered the kitchen.

"Good morning, sweetie," I offered, waiting for a reaction.

"Hey." The scowl remained, his jaw muscles tight as though barely containing a deeply buried anger.

I never knew when to ask Evan how he was doing and when to simply let him be. Today, I chose to let him be, hoping he would nevertheless tell me what was wrong.

It could be any number of things, I knew. Maybe it was the thought of having to do an antibiotic nose rinse to address the newly diagnosed staph infection—a multiple antibiotic resistant coagulase negative staph, or MARCoNS, bacteria—taking up residence deep in his nasal cavities. Along with needles, Evan had a fear of drowning, and I knew that it would be an uphill battle trying to get him to comply with this new treatment.

Maybe he had looked at his social media and seen his friends enjoying their senior year of high school while he was stuck at home. Not FOMO, fear of missing out, but TMO—truly missing out.

Or maybe he'd seen the news—heard the sounds of automatic rifle fire that could easily be mistaken for a police helicopter, its blades slicing the darkness, and seen the never-ending stream of bullets ricocheting just feet in front of screaming concertgoers running every which way—and realized that last night's mass shooting in Las Vegas would be forever linked to his eighteenth birthday.

Yes, Evan had plenty of reasons to feel depressed. But it was his sudden, often unprovoked, outbursts of anger that I didn't understand. Last month's argument was only the latest in which Evan not only raised his voice to me but also glared at me with such red-hot intensity that it sent a chill down my back.

Evan grabbed a kombucha from the fridge and, without saying another word, returned upstairs.

I went over to the coffee table where I had stacked my Lyme books, grabbed the tome sitting on top—Dr. Horowitz's *Why Can't I Get Better?*—and looked up "depression" in the index. On page two, I read that depression, anxiety, and irritability were among the psychiatric symptoms experienced by those suffering from Lyme disease and its coinfections. I didn't find anything pertaining specifically to anger, so I grabbed my laptop and entered "Lyme disease angry" into the search engine. Up popped journal articles, blog posts, and news segments on "Lyme rage," describing the sudden outbursts of anger experienced by some Lyme patients. Bingo. That's exactly how I would describe Evan's outburst last month—rage.

That evening, I revisited the idea of antidepressants with Pete. I knew from our previous discussions that Pete—a pull-yourself-up-by-the-bootstraps kind of guy—thought depression was something you should be able to control by reducing stress and finding healthy ways to cope. I knew from experience that it wasn't that simple.

We were sitting companionably in the family room, Pete on the sofa and me on the glider rocker, both of us looking at our phones, when I broke the silence.

"So, I've been reading my Lyme books . . ." I began.

Pete set down his phone and looked up at me.

". . . and it turns out that depression and something they call Lyme rage are actually neurological symptoms of Lyme disease, caused by changes in the central nervous system as a direct result of the Lyme infection."

I paused.

"I'd like to start Evan on antidepressants," I declared, cutting to the chase.

"I'm concerned about the side effects," Pete stated, his forehead furrowed with concern and, if I wasn't mistaken, agitation over having this conversation again.

Pete had also done his homework, and we knew from research that some children and adolescents had increased suicidal thoughts while taking an antidepressant.

"But I'm more worried about his mental health if he *doesn't* take an antidepressant," I explained, reminding him of the pros and cons of either decision. "Besides," I continued, "given his age and body size, he's more adult than adolescent."

Pete looked like a deer caught in headlights, as he often did when I shared a strong opinion undergirded by solid logic and references to research findings. I stopped pressing and waited for him to say something.

"I think he just needs to exercise more; then he'll feel better," Pete insisted, his voice low as he leaned toward me in earnest, his elbows resting on his knees.

"Maybe," I conceded, "once he can get out of bed. But he needs to crawl before he can walk—literally! I'm talking just for a little while to jumpstart his mood, so he can do the things he needs to, including exercise, that will help him in the long run."

Pete said nothing, but his furrowed brow had softened to a wrinkle, and his otherwise calm demeanor told me he was considering what I'd said.

I tried a different tack. "Pete, you know I take an antidepressant for depression and anxiety, and you know how much it has helped me."

In my forties, I realized with the help of therapy that I had been struggling with high-functioning depression and anxiety my entire life. I had coped by keeping busy and continuing to push forward, as if ignoring my pain would make it go away. It wasn't until the mood swings of menopause affected my relationships at home and at work that I decided it was time to consider medication.

"Have I ever told you what depression feels like?" I asked Pete. "Not the symptoms, but what it actually feels like?"

"I don't think so." Pete leaned back against the cushioned sofa and met my eyes.

"I remember one day clearly. I was driving somewhere, probably to the grocery store or Target. I was simply going through the motions, almost robotic. I felt empty and emotionless—just sort of flat, like I was watching my life on TV and not really living it. I remembered thinking, 'Why bother? What does any of this matter?'"

I glanced at Pete. He was studying my face. I continued. "And I know you remember the times when I've yelled at you or the boys in anger disproportionate to the situation. That's a symptom of anxiety."

Pete came over and leaned down to give me a hug. I stood and embraced him, then pulled back to meet his eyes. "Pete, depression is a chemical imbalance, and it can be genetic. I know my mother was depressed. Add Lyme disease to the mix, and it's no wonder Evan has bouts of depression and hopelessness."

"Well, I'm still not a fan," Pete conceded, "but I guess it wouldn't hurt for Evan to try it for a short period of time to see if it helps."

"Thank you. I know it will."

We kissed briefly, then held each other for a prolonged hug.

"Now we just need to get Evan on board," I said as we separated.

I picked up my cell phone and emailed Dr. Afrooz, sharing my concerns about Evan's mental health. She agreed to check in with Evan at his next appointment.

I was a little nervous and feeling more than just a little duplicitous when the phone rang a week later.

"How are you feeling these days?" Dr. Afrooz asked Evan.

"Uh, I still have headaches and fatigue."

"How is the parasite treatment protocol going?"

Evan looked at me quizzically. He had stopped trying to keep track of which medicines he was taking and for which ailment.

"He's been pretty good about taking his medication," I replied for him.

"And, Evan, how is your mood?" Dr. Afrooz asked without missing a beat.

"Okay, I guess."

Dr. Afrooz asked about symptoms that I recognized from research were indicators of depression. Evan answered yes to many of them.

"Would you be open to trying an antidepressant, even for a short time?" Dr. Afrooz asked.

"Sure." Evan shrugged as if to say: *Why not?*

Well, that was easy. I breathed a sigh of relief.

Chapter 20

January 2018

Pete and I lay in bed—he was reading, and I was playing Candy Crush. A wintry wind rattled our shutters, and I burrowed into the soft down comforter.

I heard a ding and looked over at my phone. I never used to take my cell phone to bed with me, but since Evan's illness, I wanted to make sure I'd see his texts requesting water or food or headache medicine at any time of the day or night.

But the text wasn't from him. It was from my best friend, Allison. I read the brief text, then smiled and turned to Pete.

"Allison is inviting me to visit her. Do you mind if I go?"

I had met Allison in 1992 at Penn State, where we were pursuing our PhDs in human development and family studies. We hit it off instantly and became kindred spirits. We were both from large families, and we shared a curiosity about family dynamics, sibling relationships, and child development. Intelligent, loving, and a free spirit, Allison was one of the most authentic people I'd ever known. We'd kept in touch over the years, visiting each other periodically as we navigated marriage, parenting, and busy careers. Recently, she and her husband had moved from the Boston area to a small town in North Carolina's Great Smoky Mountains.

Pete looked up from his book, placing his finger where he left off.

"Of course not. Tell them I say hi." He leaned over and kissed my cheek. "And don't worry about us. We'll be fine."

What would I do without Pete and his steadfast love and support? I banished the thought before my brain took that question seriously and generated scenarios of overwhelm, emotional paralysis, and loneliness.

A week later, with a suitcase in one mittened hand and a large black coffee in the other, I kissed Pete and Evan goodbye and headed out.

The nine-hour drive passed uneventfully—blissfully, even, alone with my thoughts and no one who needed me. I had forgotten what it was like not to be constantly thinking, constantly doing. Trying to prevent or solve problems. Worrying that whatever I did was somehow not enough. In this moment, however, all I needed to do was drive.

I took a deep, cleansing breath and looked out the window. The highway wound like a ribbon around the rolling hills, plush with sturdy pines undeterred by the cold that had stripped its deciduous cousins of their leaves months ago. The rising sun was orange in the morning mist and low on the horizon, throwing slanted shadows of the cars, the trees, and the foothills of the Blue Ridge Mountains. I found a smooth jazz radio station and tapped my fingers on the steering wheel as I cruised down the road.

I pulled up at Allison's back door in the late afternoon. She ran out to greet me, her boots crunching on a crisp layer of newly fallen snow. We hugged, and time melted away. I heard a familiar voice calling out "Sheroni!" as Allison's husband, Larry, appeared at the door. I smiled upon hearing his decades-old nickname for me. With long hair and a greying *Duck Dynasty*-like beard, Larry wrapped me in a bear hug; then the three of us went inside.

This was my first time at their new home, and Allison was giddy while showing me around. The front door opened into a large space with vaulted wood beam ceilings. To the left was the living room, demarcated by two puffy reclining sofas placed in an L around a huge stone fireplace, currently aglow and spreading warmth throughout the vast but cozy room. Straight ahead was the modest kitchen, and I listened as Allison described the updates they had made, including adding a beautiful island made of wood and a black granite countertop. In the far corner was the dining room—or more aptly, the breakfast nook—containing the square ceramic-top table I remember from their home outside Boston. The nook overlooked an expansive backyard that sloped down to a large lake surrounded by rows upon rows of peaks from the Great Smokey Mountains.

I stood gaping, then turned to Allison, who was beaming.

"This is beautiful! It must be so relaxing seeing this view every day!"

Next, Allison led me to the guest room and placed my suitcase on a chair. It was an inviting space with motorcycle memorabilia scattered about, including a motorcycle lamp that doubled as an alarm clock on the nightstand. Allison was all too happy to show me how it roared to life at the preset time. Thankfully, I wouldn't need an alarm clock, so I made sure it was switched off before leaving the room.

Finally, Allison showed me their newly renovated bathroom—the glazed tree stump stool catching my eye—and explained how to use the rain shower.

"But now," she announced, "I imagine you could use a nice hot bath after your long drive."

She lit the candles that adorned the sink and the tub and pulled out a box of scented bath salts, inviting me to choose whichever ones I wanted.

I rarely took baths, but as I soaked in the hot, rose-scented water, I wondered why. I vowed to change that when I got home.

Dressed in sweatpants and a flannel shirt, I rejoined Allison and Larry in the kitchen, the steaming hot chicken cordon bleu already on the table. We caught up over dinner, laughing and recalling fun times together at Penn State.

"How's Evan doing?" Larry asked between forkfuls of the savory meal.

"On the upswing, we think." It was my standard reply these days when I wasn't sure what else or how much I wanted to say.

Larry waited as if expecting me to continue. When I didn't, he simply nodded and changed the subject, updating me on what their adult daughters were up to.

Eventually, Larry said good night, and Allison and I made our way to the living room, glasses of red wine in hand, and seated ourselves on pillows in front of the blazing fire. She reached over and touched my hand.

"How *is* Evan doing?"

I took a sip of wine, enjoying the warmth that spread through my body as I thought about how to answer.

"Physically, his headaches are less frequent, and he can now concentrate long enough to do schoolwork. He's finally starting to get out of the house—he sometimes walks the dogs with Pete, and he's gotten together a couple times with a few friends from school. He even made it to Pete's parents' house for Christmas Eve!"

Evan had almost toppled over when his six-year-old cousin, Colin, launched himself into Evan's arms, having not seen him for over a year—not for Thanksgiving, or Easter, or last Christmas, and not for the many family birthday parties in between, including Evan's eighteenth birthday.

"Is Evan still sick?" Colin would inevitably ask when we showed up to family gatherings without him. "Yes," we would say, the look of disappointment clear on Colin's face, followed on one occasion by, "Will he be better when I'm twelve?" The memory still caused me to choke up.

"That's great!" Allison beamed at the good news.

"It is, but then he's wiped out and spends the next few days in bed."

I swirled my glass, watching the wine cling briefly to the sides, then slowly drain back to the bottom.

"I wish he were more consistent with his schoolwork, though." I shifted on the stone hearth. "He'd be on a roll and get a lot done, but then days would pass when he did nothing. It wouldn't be so bad if his grades didn't drop simply for slowing down." I told her about the glitch in the grade calculations that continued to mar his true progress and grades.

"That must be so frustrating for him."

"It is." Then, after a pause, "And for me!"

With anyone else, I would have felt selfish, uncaring even, admitting my impatience with my sick child. But Allison was the most emotionally secure person I knew, which made it easy to open up to her and not worry about how she was going to react. I could share the good and the bad about myself, and I knew that I would never be judged or rejected for it.

"Do you think it's more important that Evan finishes quickly or at his own pace?"

I took a long sip of wine, considering the question. I knew how Allison would answer; she had always provided her girls with the freedom to find their own ways, providing guidance and emotional support in whatever they chose to do. I wished I had her faith that my boys would be fine with more hands-off parenting, but I knew from my childhood that that was not always true.

"He doesn't need to finish quickly," I began. "I just don't want him to get used to a languid pace. I've always believed that children respond to expectations, whether high or low, and I don't want to set the bar so low that Evan comes to believe that's all he is capable of. It's Evan's goal to graduate this June with his friends, and I just want to help him reach that goal."

Allison nodded.

I stared into the fire, hypnotized by the dancing gas flames and the decorative volcanic rocks that refused to burn.

A thought tickled the back of my brain like a buzzing fly, and I swatted at it, but it refused to leave me alone. Was it really about expectations, or did the thought of Evan not making progress terrify me? It wasn't so much about forward progress, I answered myself, but about not giving up.

"You're a good momma," Allison said, ripping me from this sudden insight. Her matter-of-fact tone suggested she was stating a fact, not an opinion.

"Thank you, Ally."

"Just try to hold on," she encouraged. "This will all be over one day."

Not necessarily, I thought, remembering the stories of long-term Lyme sufferers from my Lyme support group, some of whom had been battling Lyme disease for decades. I shuddered.

"And how are you doing?" Allison continued as if sensing a need to change the subject. "How's your kidney?"

Allison knew about my family's history of chronic kidney disease and that I was now in Stage 4.

"Holding steady," I replied. "I just joined a university study researching inherited kidney diseases."

I told her about last fall's email from a cousin who had been diagnosed with kidney disease a couple of years earlier. Her father—my mother's youngest brother—had told her that the family disease was passed down only through females, which meant that he couldn't be a carrier, so she and her sister couldn't get the disease. Naturally then, my cousin was shocked by her diagnosis. But she was also intrigued. She began researching the genetics of kidney disease and found a nephrologist at Wake Forest University who was leading a research study on inherited kidney diseases.[10] She enrolled in the study and encouraged family members to do the same.

"I did the blood work a few weeks ago, and I'll find out next month if I have one of the inherited gene mutations they're studying."

Allison leaned over and gave me a hug. "When you need a transplant," she clasped my hands in hers and met my eyes, "let me know how I can get tested to be a donor."

I stared at her in stunned silence. What an unexpected offer of utter unselfishness. "Thank you," I murmured.

I returned from North Carolina with renewed optimism and perspective. And, I hoped, greater patience.

Chapter 21

March 2018

A beam of sunlight caught my half-opened eyes. The damp breeze through the open bedroom window carried the sweet, loamy scent of spring, which brought to mind pastel flowered dresses, Easter bonnets, white gloves, and my siblings and I bundled in winter coats and crammed into our faux-wood paneled station wagon on our way to Easter Mass. The added pageantry and the promise of renewal—in nature and for humanity—always made Easter feel special. I sighed. Easter was next week, and despite a half-hearted promise to myself, I knew I would not attend church services. The thought of being surrounded by people brimming with a hope that I did not share left me feeling empty.

My optimism from just two short months ago took a nose dive last week when the doctor leading the inherited kidney disease study at Wake Forest University called to inform me that I did, in fact, have one of the rare gene mutations they were studying—a mutation that didn't just increase the likelihood of kidney disease but guaranteed it. Not a matter of if but when my kidneys would fail. Confirming that this family disease was genetic felt as though a lurking enemy had finally burst from the forest to reveal itself.

I rolled over and glanced at the clock. Vigilant for any movement, Champer and Brady scampered around the bed excitedly, ready for breakfast.

"All right. Calm down."

I sat up. My shoulder muscles felt tight. Did I sleep funny? Or maybe I overdid it at the gym yesterday?

Champer was now running in circles and jumping high into the air. Brady, whining with anticipation, tried to mimic his brother, but his bulky Beagle body wouldn't cooperate. Usually, their antics amused me, but this morning, I found it irritating.

I slid into my slippers and went downstairs, careful not to trip over my exuberant dogs as they skittered past me on the stairs. I let them outside to do their business, then went to the bin of dog food under the end table in the family room. I leaned over to unsnap the handle. The tightness that originated in my shoulders had now moved to my chest, pressing on my lungs and making it difficult to breathe. Suddenly, I felt a warm tingling down my left arm, and I began to feel lightheaded.

Oh my God. Am I having a heart attack?

Determined not to pass out, I slowly climbed the stairs and knocked on Evan's door.

"What?" he answered, sleepy and clearly annoyed.

"Evan, I don't feel well. If I pass out, will you call 911?"

I heard Evan jump out of bed. He opened the door and immediately grabbed hold of me, his face etched with fear.

"Just help me lie down and bring my phone so I can call Dad."

He walked me to my bedroom where, once I lay down, I felt the tightness and dizziness begin to pass. I dialed Pete's work number and got his voicemail. I left a message saying simply I wasn't feeling well and could he come home.

Next, I called my next-door neighbor and got his voicemail.

"Hey, Rick. I don't know if I'm having a heart attack, but I can't reach Pete. I don't know what to do."

Do I wait for Pete or Rick to call me back? Should I call 911? I was already starting to feel a little better, so maybe I do nothing?

There was a knock at the front door, then in walked my neighbor.

"Where's your mom?" I heard Rick ask Evan as I made my way downstairs.

"I think I'm okay. I'm probably just dehydrated."

"I'm taking you to the emergency room," Rick declared.

I started to object. I was embarrassed, and I didn't want people fawning over me at the ER if it turned out to be nothing.

"Let's go," Rick said, letting me know that it wasn't up for debate.

During the ten-minute drive, I explained what had happened and told him I couldn't reach Pete. Rick offered to call him when we arrived at the hospital to let him know what was going on.

Thirty minutes later, as the electrocardiogram (ECG) technician was placing wires on my body, the curtains parted and Pete entered, his face ashen. Waiting for the technician to finish before he could approach me, he looked small and helpless, his furrowed brow conveying both worry and impatience. His quiet presence immediately calmed me, and I smiled weakly, giving him two thumbs up. What would I do without him, my rock? Electrodes in place, the technician stepped aside, and Pete came over and gently hugged my wired body. I explained what had happened.

"I was so worried when I got your message," Pete said, his voice quivering.

I melted into his hug. He stood by my side for the next eight hours. Three ECGs and numerous blood tests later, the ER doctor diagnosed me with sinus bradycardia—a very low heart rate—and told me to follow up with a cardiologist in two weeks. The cardiologist confirmed that I did not have a heart attack, just an irregular heartbeat.

Irregular, indeed. My heart soared with delight when Evan appeared to be getting better but then pinched in pain with each new setback. Like being flattened by ocean waves, I barely had time to catch my breath and right myself before another wave hit.

I knew I couldn't continue like this. My constant fear about Evan's health was now affecting my health.

Chapter 22

April 2018

If I had to pick one thing that got me through my parents' divorce, it would be the Serenity Prayer:

> God, grant me the serenity to accept the things I cannot change,
> the courage to change the things I can, and
> the wisdom to know the difference.

As a young adult, I concentrated on the second line, focusing with fierce intentionality on things I could control. Where I worked. Who I dated. How I spent my free time. Life was too short to worry about things I couldn't control.

Then I became a parent, and my boundless love for my children led me to worry about everything. Their safety. Their physical health. Their mental health. How they were doing in school. Who they hung out with. But the paralyzing reality was that I could do only so much to protect them from the dangers and cruelties of this world.

The only thing that provided lasting comfort was my belief in a higher power, a parental figure who loved me no matter what, who provided comfort and wisdom when life's challenges became overwhelming.

Like me, Pete was raised Catholic and went to Mass each week as a child. As parents, Pete and I likewise believed that church attendance would be important for our children's moral development, as reflected in the teachings, the example, and the loving spirit of Jesus. So after Matthew was born, we began attending Mass at a local high school auditorium in our fast-growing community.

It was a large congregation, and aside from quietly nodding "hello" to friends likewise trying to wrangle and hush their toddlers and preschoolers, it felt very impersonal. The stern priest often glared at noisy children, and his homilies typically focused on our sinful unworthiness of God's love. Church was no longer the peaceful refuge it had been during the uncertainty of my childhood years, and the pure faith I'd experienced as a child had become tainted with the reality of an imperfect institution whose rules increasingly made no sense to me and whose harsh judgment in the name of God only compounded my feelings of unworthiness and shame.

Still, throughout my adult years, I had been able to focus on the positive aspects of Catholicism—the belief in something bigger than myself, the idea that even the worst sinner can be redeemed, and the love that Jesus showed everyone, especially the poor and outcast.

But when Matthew was due to make his First Communion—a rite of passage in Catholicism in which second graders received the blessed communion wafer for the first time and began their formal instruction in Catholic doctrine—I finally had to address my ambivalence. I did not support certain Catholic doctrines, such as their stance on homosexuality and prohibitions against female, gay, and married priests, so I couldn't commit to raising my children in the Catholic Church.

So, at the age of forty, I decided to find a Christian church that better fit my understanding and experience of God's unconditional love. Pete had been supportive, confident that our boys would obtain the moral guidance we sought for them in whatever faith tradition we chose. We began attending the Church of the Holy Comforter, an Episcopal church a few towns away whose message of "All Are Welcome" had resonated with Pete and me.

The rector, Father Rick, was soft-spoken with kind eyes. He made the weekly bible readings come alive, and his sermons deftly conveyed their continued relevance in today's world. Hearing him speak was like being wrapped in a blanket and being told everything would be okay. I had treasured that weekly hour of quiet and reflection, comforted by bible stories of Hebrews and Christians weathering the storms of life with God by their sides.

I had been crushed when Father Rick announced his retirement two years ago, just as Pete and I were starting to grapple with Evan's Lyme diagnosis. Father Rick's leaving had felt like a small death, and despite the support from parishioners who inquired about Evan's health and told us they were praying for him, attending church no longer was the comfort it once had been, and we stopped going.

Instead, I tried meditating on bible verses that used to comfort me. "Do not let your heart be troubled, and do not let it be afraid"[11] had always been one of my favorites. Or the ancient wisdom of St. Julian of Norwich, whose mystic visions during a serious illness led her ultimately to conclude that "all shall be well, all shall be well, and all manner of things shall be well."[12] But now, those words leapt about my mind like rabbits: difficult to grasp and impossible to hold onto.

I hadn't lost my faith; I had experienced too many remarkable moments of joy and serendipity in my life to let a setback—even as significant as Evan's health—make me question my core beliefs in an all-loving higher power.

Still, I didn't *feel* my faith. Serendipitous moments, synchronous events, and chance encounters with strangers who left an indelible mark had always felt like a higher power directing me to where I needed to go. The sense that I was not alone in my suffering. The reassurance that the weight of the world did not, in fact, rest on my weary shoulders. I missed the feeling of a deeper connection—the kind of connection that could only be found in a community that shared my hopeful view of the world, especially during this time of personal and political upheaval.

Each year, our church offered a retreat in the fall for all parishioners and separate men's and women's retreats in the spring. Those weekends in the Shenandoah Mountains offered spiritual programs, various forms of prayer and meditation, and nature hikes during the day; informal porch fellowship with drinks and snacks in the evenings; and a Sunday morning service in the small but charming open-air cathedral built with stones from the surrounding mountains in 1925. I'd attended almost every women's retreat since coming to the Church of the Holy Comforter nearly fifteen years ago and had always come away feeling refreshed, with renewed faith, new and deepened friendships, and a new sense of perspective about life's challenges.

"Would you mind if I went to the women's retreat?" I asked Pete one Saturday morning, the open windows inviting in a warm spring breeze and the sounds of chirping birds and laughing children.

We had been sitting companionably in the family room, Pete scrolling through news websites on his phone while I played online games, when an email notification caught my eye, alerting me to the dates and registration materials for the women's retreat in two weeks.

"Not at all. I think it would do you good to get away."

"Evan could probably use some time away from me too," I remarked, laughing half-heartedly. I was only half-joking.

I could tell Pete was weighing whether to treat my remark seriously or as a joke. "He's fine," was all he said. Wise man.

It was late afternoon when I arrived in the bucolic town of Orkney

Springs, Virginia, breathtakingly beautiful with its budding trees and crocuses poking through the wet grass still patched with melting snow. I passed the old-fashioned five-and-dime store, which sold my favorite candy from the 1970s—pop rocks, bottle caps, and Charleston Chews—eliciting happy memories from an otherwise turbulent time in my life.

Rising in front of me was the nineteenth-century white clapboard building that was formerly a hotel; its four stories and floor-to-ceiling windows framed by faded green shutters drew my eyes upward to North Mountain and beyond. I rolled down the window and heard the burbling spring that gave this town its name and took a deep, cleansing breath of the crisp mountain air.

I parked my car and picked up my phone to text Pete that I had arrived safely, but I had no signal. I had forgotten that this mountain paradise lacked cell service everywhere except inside the old hotel and at the lookout on top of North Mountain. I had hoped to check the results from Evan's latest blood work as soon as they were posted but was surprised that rather than frustration, I felt a wave of relief that I could truly distance myself from Evan's illness for an entire weekend.

I ascended the hotel's wooden steps, smiling and nodding hello to a white-haired couple perched on the gleaming white Adirondack rocking chairs adorning the wide wraparound porch. In the lobby, yellow folders containing nametags, the weekend itinerary, and other information were neatly arrayed on a small table. I recognized the petite woman sitting behind the table from church, but I couldn't place her name. She smiled brightly, her clear blue eyes complementing her silver-gray hair, and handed me my folder with a sincere "Welcome!" then pointed me toward the four-bedroom cottage across the street that I would share with three other parishioners.

I rolled my small suitcase across the gravel road and entered the cottage. It smelled musty, and I instinctively worried about the mold and mildew that likely lurked behind the old wooden walls. The small living room was anchored at one end by a stone fireplace and contained a well-worn but comfortable-looking sofa and a couple of Victorian-style chairs upholstered in a flowered fabric with muted shades of red and amber. The setting was inviting, and I smiled as I approached the stairs. Four small rooms were arrayed around the landing at the top of the stairs, and I found an unclaimed room—austere with its narrow bed, single nightstand, small desk, and wooden chair—and dropped off my bags.

I had fully intended to go to the opening session, but now that I had settled in, I craved the solitude of my room and the distraction of an engaging novel. Climbing into bed, I folded the too-flat pillow against the wall, pulled the Army surplus blanket up to my chin, and began reading. The sun was just setting when I fell asleep to the sounds of peeper frogs and the quiet laughter of women enjoying wine and snacks on their front porches.

The retreat theme was "restoration of faith," and after an engaging presentation the next morning, the retreat leader handed out a large plastic bag containing those bendable, wax-coated strips of yarn found in craft stores.

"Take a handful of these sticks," she directed, "and create something that reflects where you are spiritually at this moment."

I had no idea what to do. I glanced at the other women; some exchanged puzzled glances and nervous giggles while others dove right in. I stole a peek to see what they were doing. *No cheating*, I admonished myself. I closed my eyes, took a deep breath, and asked myself, *Where am I spiritually right now?*

Fifteen minutes later, retreat participants were sharing their creations and their stories. I raised my hand to go next.

"This piece"—I pointed to a single string that I had shaped into peaks and valleys—"represents my life before my teenage son's Lyme diagnosis. There were ups and downs, but nothing I couldn't manage." I took a deep breath. "Then Evan got sick, and I quit my job to take care of him."

I scanned the room and saw sad shakes of the head and a few damp eyes telling me I was not alone in worrying about a loved one's health. "He's not getting better. And with everything going on in our country right now—the hate, the divisiveness, the violence—I'm just sad and angry and afraid all the time."

This time, there were nods. Of recognition, of compassion, of agreement. "And this"—I pointed to a jumble of multicolored waxy sticks that I had crushed into a ball—"is where I am spiritually, right now. I am stuck in a blob, uncertain of what the future holds."

When I finished, a woman whom I barely knew sitting next to me clasped my hand in solidarity. I looked over, and she smiled knowingly, revealing both laugh lines and worry lines that suggested a life well lived, full of both joy and pain.

One by one, the other women showed their creations and described how they represented their current spiritual state.

The session ended with a poem by Mary Oliver called "I Worried," read by our retreat leader.

The poem began with the author ruminating about things that could go wrong—things over which she had no control, like the flow of a river and the rotation of the earth—and fretting about how she'd be able to fix them.

I chuckled quietly, recognizing myself in those words of disquiet, revealing a need to take charge.

The retreat leader's voice became softer, almost somber, as she read the author's reflections on whether she would be forgiven—for what, she did not say, and I wondered if she was referring to something she had done or something she had failed to do. The poem ended with the author realizing that worrying had gotten her nowhere, so she stops and, instead, goes out into the day to sing. A bible verse in which Jesus encourages his disciples to have faith came to me just then: "And which of you by worrying can add a single hour to your span of life?"[13]

"Go now, into the afternoon, and sing!" the retreat leader exclaimed, entreating us to enjoy our free time before dinner.

Some friends invited me to join them on a hike up North Mountain, but I declined, preferring to sit in the warm sun and read my book. I walked to the small pond behind the group of white clapboard cottages, grabbed one of the Adirondack chairs at the edge of the water, and opened my book.

Although the novel was engaging, I couldn't help but reflect on the previous session and its dual themes of worry and faith. I had always been a worrier. I worried that my life would go off the rails if I weren't diligent about making the right decisions. I needed to learn, to know, to be certain. It was not lost on me that I became a social science researcher to find answers and uncover knowledge that could be used to prevent crises and improve people's lives.

But if I truly had faith that things would work out—if not how I wanted, then how they were meant to—then there was no need to worry, no need to control, and no need to fear uncertainty.

I thought of Father Rick, who once quoted the writer Anne Lamott during one of his sermons: "The opposite of faith is not doubt, but certainty. Certainty is missing the point entirely. Faith includes noticing the mess, the emptiness and discomfort, and letting it be there until some light returns."[14]

I returned home from the retreat to learn that Evan had tested negative for Lyme disease for the first time since his diagnosis.

The light was beginning to return.

Chapter 23

June 2018

Evan wouldn't graduate on time, and there was nothing I could do about it.

Only recently, Evan confided in me that he had been dragging his feet about finishing high school because he was nervous about what lay ahead. "I may want to take some time off before I go to college. Maybe get a job instead," he said. "I see my friends with their driver's licenses and part-time jobs and going out with friends. I want to do that!"

Pete and I both had advanced degrees, which helped us greatly in our careers. We didn't expect Matthew and Evan to pursue graduate school necessarily, but we had expected them to attend a four-year college. It was never a question of whether, only where, the boys would go to college.

"You know, you can do those things *and* go to college," I suggested. "You can take classes at the community college—as many or as few as you want each semester."

Evan had nodded noncommittally, and I had left it at that. We had time before he needed to make any decisions about college and work. More immediately, I wanted Evan to see his school friends before they dispersed to college.

An idea hit me one afternoon.

I knocked on Evan's bedroom door, and after being invited in, I proposed the idea of attending graduation so he could see his friends. Propped up in bed with his computer on his lap—he was either doing homework or playing video games, but at that moment, I didn't care—he shrugged and quirked his lip to one side.

"I don't know, maybe," he said.

That was enough for me. I emailed his high school principal, begging him to let Evan participate in the June graduation ceremony even though he wouldn't have finished his coursework by then. I emphasized the importance of Evan being with his classmates one last time. I even played the nostalgia card, arguing that the symbolic gesture of walking at graduation would not only motivate Evan, it would also inspire his entire class—and after all, isn't that what graduation ceremonies were all about?

His principal called the next day with his decision, and I descended the basement steps to break the news to Evan.

"Evan, I heard back from Dr. Brewer. He's proud of your accomplishments given the circumstances, but he said you'd need to complete all your online coursework in order to walk at graduation."

"That's okay." Not looking up, Evan continued to shoot zombies. "I didn't want to go to graduation anyway."

But it wasn't okay for me. He was already missing out on so many opportunities—dating, getting his driver's license. Did he really not care?

I looked over at Evan and saw the five-year-old who had missed the chance to meet the legendary author Eric Carle and get his *Very Hungry Caterpillar* book autographed because we arrived too late at the Eric Carle Museum of Picture Book Art. Pete, the boys, and I had been visiting Allison and her family outside Boston, and true to form, I had tried to fit in too many activities to entertain my family, and we simply left too late. "Eric Carle is my favorite author! He's the reason I love reading!" Evan had gushed from his booster seat as I battled traffic on Interstate 90, racing my family to the museum. Upon arrival, Pete got the boys out of the car while I ran inside just as they were closing the line for autographs. I had begged them to make an exception but, of course, they couldn't. We ended up snapping a photo of Evan with Mr. Carle signing books in the background. Evan was satisfied, but I had silently cried in a bathroom stall with crushing disappointment.

"It's weird." Evan paused the game and turned to me. "I see my friends from high school going to restaurants and stuff without their parents, and I forget that they are old enough to drive. I still feel like I'm sixteen."

My heart ached for this insightful young man, for whom time stopped with his Lyme diagnosis. I took a seat next to him and met his eyes.

"I know it's hard right now, honey. You've experienced difficulty early in your life, but believe me, things will get better. It might actually lead to something positive, like, maybe you'll be a teacher who understands students with chronic illnesses or a doctor who treats Lyme disease."

Evan looked down, shaking his head slowly, almost imperceptibly, and heaved a sigh that may have been a quiet sob.

"Or a computer programmer who designs educational software..."

His face softened as the corner of his lips slowly curled into a smile. He looked at me, and we both chuckled.

"In any event, this experience will only make you more compassionate of others and give you the resilience necessary to lead a fulfilling life."

God, please let that be true, I prayed, knowing that not everyone bounced back from adversity.

A few days later, as I was plopping dry pasta into boiling water for that night's dinner, Evan emerged from the basement, humming a catchy tune. I asked him what he was singing.

"It's new from Panic! At The Disco. It's called 'High Hopes.'"

I liked the name of the song, and I especially liked that Evan liked it.

"Check this out." He cued up the song on his cell phone, and I listened to Evan croon that he was going to be one in a million.

I smiled, grateful for the power of music.

"So . . ." Evan stared at the floor, jiggling his leg. "Emily and Annie texted me about going to prom."

I remained calm, knowing any sudden move or show of excitement might scare this critter back into his hole. "That's nice." I continued to chop basil.

"They said it would be fun for the three of us to go together and that I could find a tie that matched both their dresses."

"That does sound like fun. Do you think you want to go?" I tried desperately to keep the excitement out of my voice. I wanted it to be his decision, with no influence from me.

"You know I don't like to plan things because I never know how I'm gonna feel. If I plan on going but then don't, I'll be more upset than if I didn't plan to go in the first place."

I marveled at Evan's self-awareness and his ability to clearly communicate what he was thinking and feeling. I nodded but said nothing. Chop. Chop. Chop.

"But I figure if I rest up before and after, I could probably manage it."

Hallelujah!

"Sounds good," I replied, aiming unsuccessfully for detached indifference.

The evening of prom arrived, rainy but not at all dreary. The girls arrived moments apart, and Evan met them at their cars with an umbrella.

Rays of sun poked through the dark clouds as if the weather, too, were unsure how the evening would go.

Annie looked regal in her royal-blue satin gown, and Emily was elegant in a pale-green vintage-style dress. As planned, Evan wore a royal-and-sage plaid tie that matched their dresses perfectly. The girls had insisted on making their own corsages so that they'd match the boutonnieres—one royal, one sage—they had made for Evan. The trio donned their flowers and posed for pictures in our sunroom, the glistening green trees providing the perfect backdrop.

When it was time to meet their friends at the Japanese restaurant they had selected, I hugged Evan and the girls goodbye and thanked Emily's mother for agreeing to drive them. The night was starting out better than I could have hoped. I poured a glass of my favorite sauvignon blanc and took a seat next to Pete on the sofa. He greeted me with a kiss on the cheek. I pulled up the photos I had just taken on my phone, and Pete placed his arm on my shoulders and pulled me closer as we scrolled through images of our dapper young man, his smile frozen in time.

Pete and I spent the evening watching TV, our cell phones nearby with the ringers on. I was grateful for each passing hour that we didn't get a call or text from Evan. "I'll probably just stay an hour or two," Evan had said, but as it approached 10:00 p.m., we still hadn't heard from him. In a daring "screw you" to the boogeyman of despair, I allowed myself to hope.

At midnight, Pete finally received Evan's text to pick him up. Pete returned twenty minutes later but without Evan. Before I could express concern, I saw Pete's smile.

"I dropped Evan and his friends at IHOP. He'll text when he's ready to be picked up."

I was near tears—happy tears this time—grateful that Evan had been able to experience this quintessential high school rite of passage.

It almost made up for all the other high school moments he'd missed. Almost.

Evan texted Pete around 1:00 a.m., requesting to be picked up. Minutes later, they walked through the front door. Evan looked both exhausted and elated.

"So, how was it?" I asked, barely containing my excitement. I glanced at Pete, whose ear-to-ear smile told me he had already gotten the rundown on the ride home.

"It was great!" Evan beamed, pacing the family room as he recounted the evening. "My friends came up to me throughout the night telling me how good it was to see me!"

"And how was your energy?" I took in every word, every gesture with delight.

"It was good!" Evan was now bouncing on his toes like a bird about to take flight. "I danced for a few songs . . . they had a really good DJ . . . he played 'Party in the USA,' and everyone went crazy! . . . and then, yeah . . . I'd take breaks when I got tired."

His stream-of-consciousness response reminded me of how he used to babble frenetically as an overtired toddler.

Soon, the adrenaline drained from Evan's body, and he said good night. With the clomp-clomp of dress shoes, he lumbered up the stairs, a sleepy smile spreading wide on his face. The night felt both normal and extraordinary. I rested my head on Pete's chest and clung to this feeling of hope.

Chapter 24

October 2018

The theater lights dimmed, and the chittering crowd quieted, the anticipation as intense as the smell of buttered popcorn. I gripped Pete's hand, readying myself for the jump scares that I knew were coming. To my right, Matthew and Evan were feigning fear while trying to freak each other out with an unseen hand grabbing the other's shoulder or leg. Suddenly, the word "HALLOWEEN" filled the screen as the opening notes of John Carpenter's iconic score—DOO-doo-doo DOO-doo-doo DOO-doo-doo DEE-doo—echoed throughout the theater. Three little notes, deceptively simple but effective in resurrecting images from the original movie forty years ago and my terrified reactions as a fourteen-year-old. It's funny how the slightest reminder can trigger memories from the past.

Going to the new *Halloween* movie and ordering takeout from his favorite pizza place were the only presents Evan wanted for his nineteenth birthday. Again this year, he chose not to attend the large family get-together to celebrate his and his two cousins' birthdays at his aunt's house, a ninety-minute drive away. Although he was beginning to feel better, when he did go out, he did not wander far from home in case he needed to lie down and rest.

He didn't even want cake and ice cream, having finally been convinced that eating sugar only served to feed the bacteria, viruses, and fungal infections that we were trying to kill. I didn't know if it was my endless lectures or if he had discovered for himself that he felt better when he ate healthier foods. Either way, I was grateful that there were fewer arguments and greater progress in his health, schoolwork, and social life.

In August, Evan had tested negative for mycotoxins for the first time in two years. "You made my day!" Dr. Afrooz had exclaimed when she saw those results. And although he continued to test positive for Rocky Mountain spotted fever, his titers were holding steady at 1:128—still elevated, but an improvement over its peak of 1:256 a year ago. Dr. Afrooz had explained that antibody titers could remain high for months, even years, after the infection was gone, so she wasn't worried. She reiterated how important the clinical assessment of symptoms was, and because Evan's symptoms had greatly improved—suffering only periodically from joint pain and fatigue—she was very happy with Evan's progress.

With fewer symptoms, Evan had been able to tackle homework on a more regular basis. By mid-September, he had completed half of his history course and one-third of his chemistry course. Unfortunately, that meant he'd left English and Personal Finance/Economics untouched for weeks, and his progress and grades in those classes had declined. I had been tempted to remind Evan of his Sisyphean dilemma, but I bit my tongue. I didn't want to motivate him out of fear, which I recently realized I had been doing inadvertently since Evan's diagnosis.

I had decided to prioritize Evan's mental health, which had improved greatly since he began taking an antidepressant, by following his lead rather than by pushing him based on some arbitrary deadline.

I created a spreadsheet that estimated dates of completion for each course, which I projected based on the average time it took him to complete each activity and various assumptions about how many hours he spent each week doing schoolwork. I had wanted Evan to understand the direct link between how much he worked and when he could expect to finish high school. I had also hoped that seeing a daily rise in his completion rate would motivate him to keep going.

The math also helped me understand what was realistic for me to expect from Evan. After nearly three years of guiding, directing, cajoling, and outright pushing, I had finally accepted that I couldn't make Evan do his schoolwork. But I could help him choose his own deadline based on the pace that worked for him.

The audience gasped at the reveal of Michael Myers in the jail yard, and the accompanying music crescendo brought me back to the darkened theater. I looked over at Matthew and Evan, still joking and laughing, and my heart soared. I turned to Pete, who was looking at me. I suspect he had been watching me watch our boys. We smiled at each other as if to say: *We made it. Things are finally beginning to look up.*

Chapter 25

February 2019

Evan bounced from his dresser to his closet, grabbing armfuls of neatly folded clothes and stuffing them into a duffle bag. My boys had always preferred shorts to pants, even in the dead of winter, so I reminded Evan that the Blue Ridge Mountains of Virginia were especially cold in February and suggested he pack at least one pair of pants. To my surprise, he did.

I had long thought that when Evan was healthy enough, visiting Matthew at Virginia Tech would be the perfect reentry into the outside world, giving him a taste of what awaited him at college. Matthew's birthday was on Monday, and Evan was going to visit for a long weekend. Evan hadn't been to Virginia Tech since the four of us had toured colleges in Matthew's junior year of high school, over four years ago. And now here he was, packing for his trip to spend the weekend with his big brother at college.

I was both excited and nervous for him. Like finally removing the training wheels from a child's bike, I expected some wobbles, but I had faith he'd remain upright.

Evan had been enjoying increasing autonomy in the last few months. He was doing his schoolwork, taking his medicine, and going to bed at a reasonable time without any prompting from me. He also finally wanted to learn how to drive, so Pete and I took turns copiloting as Evan drove around our quiet neighborhood. After a slight freak out on my part when it appeared that Evan was about to sideswipe a neighbor's car parked on the street, even though Evan had insisted he had plenty of room, we all agreed it would be best if I taught Evan how to park in the relative safety of the high school parking lot during off-hours when it stood empty.

Pete, ever the rock of calmness, took the lead on teaching Evan to drive, first on side roads, then on the main roads, then on the busy highway, navigating entry and exit ramps. With Pete copiloting from the front passenger seat, Evan safely navigated to the local coffee shop to hang out with Emily when she came home from college for winter break.

Not sure how much independence he wanted, I had offered to drive Evan to Virginia Tech, but I also mentioned it might be fun to take the bus by himself. I had been thrilled when he had opted to spend a total of eight hours in the car with his ole mom. The plan was to drop him off in Blacksburg, then I'd continue to North Carolina to visit my bestie, Allison, then pick him up on my way back home.

On the ride down, I asked what he and Matthew were going to do.

"No set plans," Evan said, then turning to me, "you know I don't like to plan." His deadpan expression could not hide the twinkle in his eye, referring playfully to the arguments we used to have about the importance of planning for getting things done.

I met his eyes and smiled, catching the joke. This gentle teasing was our family's way of telling each other we were sorry, forgiving each other, and leaving hurt feelings in the past.

"Matthew put together a list of ideas," Evan continued, a smile now spread wide on his face. "Restaurants, hiking trails, and other stuff."

I assumed this "other stuff" was what he'd have been doing without my knowledge if he were away at college, so I decided not to press him for details.

"Sounds like fun!"

I stole another glance at my son. He'd gained back all the weight he had lost three years ago, and his hefty frame sat upright in the passenger seat, his round face now sporting a full mustache and beard.

Gradually, Evan's smile faded, and he turned serious. "Mom, what if I feel sick when I'm there?"

Poor kid. Always afraid of what might be lurking around the corner.

"Same as you do here. Rest, drink lots of water, and take your meds."

Evan was still taking immune supplements, a multivitamin, an antidepressant, and another round of doxycycline that we had hoped would finally knock out the RMSF bacteria that seemed to be lingering in his body.

"Pack Excedrin in case you get a migraine," I continued. "And I'll bet Matthew could find your favorite kombucha at the grocery store so you can keep feeding your gut good bacteria."

Evan was nodding, but I could see the worry on his face.

"Honey, you'll be fine. This will be fun!" And then, recalling the "other stuff" he might be doing, I repeated the mantra they'd heard throughout their teen years: "Just keep your wits about you."

On the ride home four days later, Evan was utterly glowing.

"Matthew's friends are so nice! I didn't know how they'd feel about Matthew's kid brother tagging along, but they treated me like an equal! Matthew's roommate called me 'Little Matt' all weekend!"

Evan was bouncing in his seat and making elaborate gestures with his hands. His wide eyes alternated between glancing at me and staring out the window as if watching a replay of the weekend's events. He looked like an animatronic bobblehead doll.

"We played video games, did an escape room, and a bunch of us shot hoops at one in the morning on the basketball court outside Matthew's apartment."

"How were you feeling?"

"I rested all day while they were in class, then we hung out and did things at night and on the weekend. It all worked out fine!"

I couldn't remember the last time I had seen Evan this happy. "A mother is only as happy as her least happy child"—isn't that how the saying goes? In this moment, I was the happiest mother on earth.

And I was no longer afraid that Evan would sink into a pool of despair.

Chapter 26

March–May 2019

A couple of weeks after he returned from visiting Matthew, Evan had a phone appointment with Dr. Afrooz—his first appointment since last October. When Evan's health had begun improving in 2018, Dr. Afrooz reduced his visits from monthly to every other month. The fact that it had now been five months since Evan's last appointment was not only a hopeful sign that he was on his way to a full recovery, but it also allowed us to live our lives without the frequent reminder of Evan's condition.

We put Dr. Afrooz on speakerphone, and she ran through the list of symptoms, which I had practically memorized by now. Headaches? Stomachaches? Fatigue? Night sweats? Dizziness or loss of balance? Difficulty concentrating?

This time, Evan answered "no" to most of them. Only periodic joint pain remained.

"Dr. Afrooz," I interrupted. "I noticed that Evan not only tested negative for Lyme disease, all of the bands on the Western blot were also negative."

She anticipated my question.

"As you know," she cautioned, "the current blood tests we have for detecting Lyme disease can't tell us if Evan is cured. But it is a good sign that all bands are negative. It's a better sign that he is nearly symptom-free."

Evan and I exchanged hopeful glances.

"In fact," Dr. Afrooz continued, the smile evident in her voice, "I would say that Evan's Lyme is in remission. His immune system has the upper hand, and his symptoms are finally under control."

I turned to Evan, expecting a dramatic fist pump or high five, but he just sat there, and for a moment, I wasn't sure he had heard her. Then I saw his eyes glisten and his shoulders sag—not in defeat this time, but in relief. He slowly turned toward me and smiled, a full smile that reached his eyes and his dimpled cheeks, and my heart soared.

Throughout April, Evan worked on his schoolwork with an intensity that surprised and delighted me. He had completed Chemistry and Personal Finance/Economics in January and had only two courses to go: English 12 and US/VA Government. He was committed to graduating in May, and I couldn't think of a better Mother's Day gift.

Despite Evan's increased motivation, his English course remained the bane of his existence. He was a good writer but believed that he didn't deserve the one hundred percent he received on many of his essays because even he could find errors. His teacher was supportive, with emails exclaiming, "Great job on your *Beowulf* quiz!" The positive feedback was lost on Evan, however: He was tired of performing beneath his abilities and having his mediocrity celebrated. As a result, he didn't care about doing his best and wanted only to finish his courses with a passing grade. As a nineteen-year-old in his fifth year of high school, I guess I couldn't blame him.

Evan finally completed English at the end of April. He was happy with his "A" but was still not convinced he'd earned it. Pete and I told him how proud of him we were, but that also fell flat with him, so our celebration was muted. I didn't mind, really. I knew the real celebration would be when he completed his final course and—finally—finished high school.

One Sunday evening in May, while Pete and I were watching *God Friended Me*, Evan came up from the basement and just stood there, a dumbfounded look frozen on his face. I set down my nightly glass of wine and looked up at him.

"Guys," he said, a slow smile starting to spread across his face, "I think I just finished history!"

We double-checked his dashboard against the information on the parent portal.

"It sure looks like you did," I exclaimed. "And you got an A!"

"Great job, Ev!" Pete and I went to Evan and gave him a hug.

"Should I email my teacher to let them know?"

Evan was now bouncing on his tippy toes—all 6' 2", 165 pounds of him—but all I saw was the little boy watching his big brother successfully open a hidden doorway and earn jewel-colored rupees in his Legend of Zelda video game.

"Yes!" I replied, my heart nearly leaping out of my chest. "Email your online teacher and CC Mrs. Amodeo, Dr. Brewer, the school district's homebound adviser, and me and Dad. Tell them you've completed the course requirements." After a pause, I added, ". . . and make sure you attach a screenshot of the history dashboard."

"I'll do that now," Evan agreed, "so they can close out the course tomorrow morning before the pacing calculation lowers my progress and grade." We exchanged exasperated smiles.

"Good thinking, Ev." I gave him another hug. "I am so proud of you and your perseverance—throughout high school. I know it's been difficult, but you did it! You should be very proud of yourself."

And just like that, with minimal fanfare, Evan was done with high school. Almost three years exactly from the date he had been diagnosed with Lyme disease.

"Thanks, guys. I can't believe I'm finally done . . ." Evan trailed off, sounding wistful for a moment. Then he bounded up the stairs, taking them two at a time.

"Hey, Matt!" he called to his brother, who had recently returned home from college for the summer. "Guess what?"

I looked above the mantel at the boys' framed school photos arrayed in a circle like a clock: the grinning kindergartners at the top, fresh with possibilities; the shaggy-haired middle schoolers in basketball jerseys at six o'clock; the pimpled teenagers at ten o'clock. For Matthew, the center space showed a smiling high school graduate in a cap and gown. For Evan, that spot stood empty. I had offered to hire a professional photographer to take his graduation picture—I even dusted off Matthew's cap and ironed his gown—but Evan had declined. I bristled slightly at the empty space, and I vowed to fill the vacancy someday soon with a current picture of Evan, smiling.

I leaned my head against Pete's shoulders and exhaled a long, slow breath, expelling three years of worry; three years of doctor's appointments, shifting medications, and experimental treatments; three years of arguments over too many hours playing video games and too few hours spent on schoolwork; three years of frustrated outbursts, hugs and apologies, improvements and setbacks interspersed with rare but treasured moments of hope.

Chapter 27

June 2019

Spring's pale-red buds gave way to summer's deep-green leaves. Pete and I continued to encourage Evan to take walks and get together with his high school friends—or his IRL (in real life) friends, as Evan calls them. We also broached the topic of what Evan wanted to do now that he had finished high school. He reiterated his interest in working part-time and going to community college part-time, so I began texting him registration information and job announcements.

"Hey, Evan! A new store just opened and they're hiring cashiers. And it's right up the road. You could walk there!"

Evan hadn't yet obtained his driver's license, so a job nearby was key.

"I was thinking about applying to that ice cream shop in the new plaza."

"And look here!" I continued as if Evan hadn't spoken. "The rec center is hiring a front desk worker. You'd check people in, hand out basketballs, maybe even help kids with the climbing wall."

Trying to anticipate his concerns while playing up the fringe benefits, I added: "You could sit if you get tired, and I'll bet you could use the workout equipment and gym if you wanted to. It would definitely provide the social interaction you're looking for!"

"Mom, just listen!" His tone was insistent but not angry. "I want to work at the ice cream store. I like that the plaza has live music on Wednesday nights, and it would be fun to serve ice cream to little kids."

I had to admit, that did sound like fun.

I stared at the young man in front of me, a twinkle of excitement in his eyes. He was ready to fly, so it was time I took off the training wheels.

"When would you like to pick up a job application?"

Evan was having a ball working at the ice cream shop. A year ago, he had been winded after walking up a flight of stairs, but now Evan could stand throughout his five-hour shifts without tiring. He was a quick learner and a hard worker, and the owner soon came to rely on him to open and close the shop and train new employees. He easily befriended his coworkers—high school and college students like himself—and they hung out together outside of work. After each shift, Evan regaled Pete and me with stories of cute kids, odd ice cream requests, and the occasional rude customer. Evan was happy and hopeful.

Chapter 28

October 2019

"Have fun! Be safe!" I called after Evan as he jogged down the driveway after a quick change out of his custard-stained T-shirt and khakis and hopped into his friend's car.

"We will. Love you!" Evan called back.

"Bye, Mom! Don't wait up!" his coworkers sing-songed out the open car windows, laughing as they drove off. It was a warm Saturday evening in October, and they were taking Evan to their favorite Peri-Peri chicken restaurant for his twentieth birthday.

I shut the front door and turned to Pete, who was still chuckling.

"He's not home five minutes before he's out the door again!" I said in mock exasperation. Actually, I was thrilled that Pete and I hardly saw Evan anymore.

In addition to hanging out with friends and working twenty hours a week at the custard store—not ice cream, Evan had continually reminded me, taking pride in both his job and their superior product— Evan was taking his first class at the community college, freshman

English. He had been nervous about what to expect from a college-level course, especially now that he no longer had nor needed special accommodations.

But from the first assignment in which students were asked to write about their goals for the future, it was clear that Evan was right where he was supposed to be.

"Because of Mrs. Amodeo's willingness to help others," his essay read, "I decided in high school that I wanted to study psychology. Her way of showing me perspective and caring for others made me want to see other people's perspectives so that I can care for them as well. To be able to give people the same guidance and support that I was given would be a dream come true, and it is something that I am willing to work hard for."

The following day, it was our turn to take Evan out for dinner. Matthew had come home from college to celebrate this double milestone birthday—Evan was no longer sick, and he was no longer a teenager. As Pete navigated the side streets of our small suburb, I fidgeted with the air conditioning from the front seat while the boys each grabbed for the auxiliary cord in an effort to control the playlist during our ten-minute drive to the restaurant. Evan won. Matthew conceded gracefully, acknowledging that "we like the same music anyway."

A single guitar's warm notes oozed out of the speakers and were soon joined by a cello and an indie rock drum beat.

Evan stared out the window, tapping his fingers on his knees almost absentmindedly.

"Great song," Pete said. Then seeing my quizzical expression, "'Cough Syrup' by Young the Giant."

I knew pop and classic rock, and Pete knew alternative rock. No wonder our boys had such varied playlists.

"You know," Evan said, still gazing into the late afternoon sun, "I used to listen to this all the time when I was sick."

I tilted my head and listened closely to the lyrics. My brow furrowed with concern as I heard the lead singer mourn about losing his mind and not caring about his life.

"It starts off kinda sad," Evan continued, returning his attention to inside the car. "He sings about not achieving his dreams. But it's kinda happy too."

I listened as Evan continued to croon the chorus, his emotions evident in his beatific face and full-throated singing about chasing dreams and restoring life.

"Why is it called 'Cough Syrup'?" I asked, now turned fully around to look at him in the back seat.

"Because," Evan said, "it's the medicine you need to get stronger, even if it doesn't taste good."

Although it was Evan's birthday, I felt like I was the one receiving gifts. The biggest gift, of course, was Evan's health. Physically, his energy was back, he weighed a robust 200—thanks to free custard samples at work—and he no longer suffered from the pain that had held him hostage for almost four years. Mentally, he could focus on homework for hours, his clever wit had returned, and he no longer felt despondent. Socially, Evan had reentered the world with gusto. He spent his free time with his friends from work and had even reconnected with old friends from high school with whom he thought he'd lost touch forever.

I also received the gift of time. Time with Evan that, although often contentious, was a true blessing. Through conflict, we better understood each other's needs and limits. We permitted each other to show our anger and frustration, knowing that our love for each other was very much intact and never at risk. We had wonderful conversations about current events—of which there were many to discuss—and why people do what they do. I watched Evan navigate some of the most difficult things a person could experience—a chronic illness, social isolation—and I watched him emerge on the other side a mature young man.

I also had the gift of time away from my fast-paced career. I read more. I cooked more. I spent more time with Pete, who had supported whatever I needed to do to cope and had made me smile at a time when I thought I would never experience laughter again.

And now, I had nothing but high hopes for the future and could not wait to see what 2020 would bring.

Chapter 29

May 2020

I peeled the living room curtains aside and stared out the window at the abandoned street. The late afternoon sun shone brightly in the cloudless sky, but there were no young children playing in their front yards, squealing with laughter. No middle schoolers playing three-on-three basketball at the curbside hoop next door. No boisterous teenagers walking down the middle of the street on their way home from school. No ever-present hum of airplanes overhead departing from or arriving at Dulles International Airport fifteen miles away. Even the birds seemed to have gone quiet.

The COVID-19 pandemic had brought the world to a screeching halt. Across the globe, stay-at-home orders had been put in place to limit the spread of this new, deadly virus. Although some doubted its severity, I was not about to play fast and loose with my health—even if that meant being stuck at home for the foreseeable future.

The only sign of life I could see was Pete wrangling our leashed dogs down the driveway for their afternoon walk. I loved that Pete was home full-time for the foreseeable future, but I felt a deep sense of unfairness that he continued to receive a paycheck while others either lost their jobs as businesses shuttered or continued to work in high-risk settings as essential workers, including nurses, doctors, police, and grocery store employees.

A lone bird flew overhead, reminding me of a desolate opening scene from one of those apocalyptic movies. It was a stark reminder that there were forces beyond our control, often invisible but too impactful to ignore, that could turn our worlds upside down, thrusting us into an uncertain future.

At least both my children were home safe, I comforted myself. Matthew had graduated from Virginia Tech in December and then returned home to look for a job. I marveled that it had been almost five years since we dropped him off at college. The memories came swimming back: Our tour of Virginia Tech and Matthew's audition for the School of Performing Arts. His excitement at being admitted early decision. His new friends. His first girlfriend. His change of majors from music technology to statistics. All his highs and lows.

Matthew had started looking for a job in January, searching online for entry-level jobs in statistics or data analysis. He had had a couple of nibbles and was in the process of following up when COVID hit. Initially, I pressed him to keep trying because, surely, this outbreak wouldn't last long. But then the number of infections, hospitalizations, and deaths soared, and it was clear that the pandemic was only going to get worse. Hiring in his field had stopped, and job announcements had dried up.

Two months into the pandemic, Matthew now spent the bulk of his time playing online video games with his friends, the only friends he regularly kept in touch with. I had to remind myself that he wasn't being lazy or irresponsible—in fact, by avoiding in-person contact with others, Matthew was being extremely responsible, and mindfully so.

Experts were learning that immunocompromised individuals and those with certain preexisting health conditions—including chronic kidney disease—were at greater risk for infection, hospitalization, and death. Less concerned about getting infected himself, Matthew didn't want to infect Evan or me.

Evan also had been worried that he might be especially susceptible to infection, given his bout with Lyme disease. Recalling the toll that those tick-borne and secondary infections had on his immune system, we had a phone appointment with Dr. Afrooz in March, with whom we hadn't spoken since she declared Evan's Lyme disease in remission over a year ago.

Dr. Afrooz had been pleased to hear from Evan and was genuinely interested in how he was doing. Evan had filled her in on his life, that he had been working at a frozen custard store until it shut down due to COVID, that he was currently studying psychology at the community college and would be transferring to Virginia Tech in the fall. Dr. Afrooz had been thrilled to hear about his plans, exclaiming, "We need more mental health professionals who understand the effects of chronic infections on mental health. We need more people like you!"

Evan had beamed at her encouragement, his chest puffed with pride, and I had thanked Dr. Afrooz for all she had done for him—medically and emotionally—over the years. Evan had then explained that he was having trouble taking a deep breath and, having learned that shortness of breath was a symptom of COVID, he wondered if he should worry. Dr. Afrooz had ordered a chest X-ray—which had come back normal—and advised him to wear a mask, socially distance in public, and start taking mega doses of vitamin C, vitamin D, and vitamin A to boost his immune system. I had worried that Evan would resist the additional blood work and having to take pills again, but he had happily agreed and diligently complied.

I turned from the window to look at Evan. Hunched over his

laptop at the dining room table, he alternately looked at the computer screen, then tappity-tapped on his keyboard. After a semester-and-a-half of in-person classes at the community college, he was back to remote learning. This young man who had conquered Lyme disease and who had endured three years of online high school classes was once again homebound.

I moved toward Evan and rested a hand on his shoulder.

"How's it going?" I asked, brushing his overgrown hair out of his eyes. He leaned slightly into my caress, suggesting that not only didn't he mind this motherly habit of mine, he actually welcomed it.

"Okay, I guess." He stopped typing and turned to face me. "It definitely feels weird that I'm stuck in the house again—finishing my classes online, not working, not going out with friends—just like when I was sick."

My stomach sank at those words, as if I'd just crested the top of a roller coaster and was now plunging down the other side. Evan must have seen my frown and stood up to give me a hug.

"But it's okay, Mom. I know things will get better, even if I don't know when."

I didn't know exactly when it happened, but my frail, frustrated, disease-ridden sixteen-year-old had matured into a healthy, responsible, wise twenty-year-old, and my heart soared with delight—despite the circumstances that gave me a front-row seat.

Chapter 30

September 2020

Fall had always been my favorite season and September my favorite month. After Labor Day, the temperatures in Northern Virginia dropped like a velvet curtain at the end of a dazzling theater performance. The summer's hazy skies of milky white gave way to crystal clear skies of deep cerulean blue. With lower humidity and daytime temperatures topping out in the seventies, I returned to the outdoors and gulped down autumn's fresh air as though I had been holding my breath all summer.

Six months into the pandemic, the average number of weekly COVID cases was on the rise again after having declined in August. Experts warned of a likely explosion of COVID cases during flu season, and I continued to worry about what that meant not only for my health and that of my family and friends but also for the health of others with compromised immune systems and the safety of essential workers.

Other than taking walks in my neighborhood—which had declined in frequency during the unbearable summer heat and humidity—I avoided public places. Pete did all the grocery shopping, fully masked and following arrows on the floor that directed the flow of foot traffic, turning aisles into one-way thoroughfares and checkout counters into broken lines with six-foot intervals between patrons.

Now that Pete's company had figured out a schedule of part-time attendance and an office plan that kept employees safely distanced from one another, he would be returning to work next month. Evan remained healthy and continued his online community college courses, while Matthew continued hanging out with his friends online, sometimes playing video games but often just talking. I had come to appreciate the social lifeline that online video games provided my boys during times of physical isolation.

Today, I sat on our back patio enjoying the warm breeze and rustling leaves, grateful that I no longer felt like a prisoner in my own home as I had during the sizzling summer. I took a sip of water from my oversized water bottle and stared at my cell phone, pondering my next guess in Wordle. A notification from my health app popped up, alerting me that the results from my blood draw last week were ready. Despite receiving dozens of such notifications over the past four years, my heart still skipped a beat, dreading what I might learn.

I opened the app and logged into my account. My finger hovered over the test results button, reminding myself that there is hope. Last year, I attended a meeting of patients participating in the Wake Forest University inherited kidney disease research study who, like me, had an Autosomal Dominant Tubulointerstitial Kidney Disease, or ADTKD. Not only did I learn more about the disease, I also found about advances being made in finding a treatment. Advances that could halt this insidious disease from further ravaging my family tree.

I took a deep breath, clicked on the test results icon and gasped. My kidney was now functioning at only twenty-two percent capacity, down from twenty-seven percent just four short months ago. This marker of kidney functioning fluctuated up or down one or two percentage points between appointments, often depending on my level of hydration. But a drop of five percentage points? Never before had my kidney functioning dropped so low or so quickly. As if making up for the skipped beat seconds before, my heart now raced.

A quick calculation told me that, at my current rate of decline, I could drop below twenty percent by the holidays, at which time I could be evaluated for a transplant. I decided not to wait that long.

"When can I start the transplant evaluation process?" The words were out of my mouth the minute Dr. Assefi and I finished exchanging pleasantries during my September tele-visit.

I desperately wanted to avoid dialysis—I had seen the toll it took on my mother and my grandmother, and for long-term survival, a transplant was necessary—which meant getting on the transplant list as soon as possible. The current wait time for a kidney in Virginia for my blood type was five to eight years, longer than the national average of three to five years.

"Normally, I wait until my patients' kidney functioning is less than twenty percent," Dr. Assefi replied, then looked off camera, examining my latest test results, I guessed. "Your current functioning is twenty-two percent . . . down from twenty-seven percent in May."

Was that concern I saw in his normally placid face?

He removed his glasses and turned back to the camera, his kind brown eyes meeting mine. "How have you been feeling, dear?"

"I'm still tired a lot of the time, even though I sleep ten to twelve hours a day." As if on cue, I stifled a yawn. "And my brain is fuzzy," I told Dr. Assefi. "I'm absentminded, and I have trouble maintaining a train of thought."

Dr. Assefi nodded, his eyes creased with sympathy, a knowing smile crossing his face. "I can refer you to the transplant center to begin testing now if you would like."

"That would be great!" I wondered if Dr. Assefi caught the hitch in my voice. "Thank you."

Since my mother was diagnosed with end-stage renal failure thirty-five years ago, I had assumed that this disease that tracked through my family would one day track me down. Years of uncertainty and anxious anticipation left me feeling like the protagonist in Edgar Allen Poe's "The Pit and the Pendulum," frantically watching an instrument of death swing ever closer to me with each passing year.

And now the day had finally come. I felt an odd mix of emotions: gratitude that I could begin the life-saving process of getting on the kidney transplant list, but sad that I needed to. Confident that I had done everything I could to take care of my health—regular nephrology appointments, maintaining a kidney-friendly diet, drinking plenty of water, staying active—but afraid that, in the end, it wouldn't matter. For now I knew that being responsible didn't guarantee that bad things wouldn't happen . . . that sometimes shit happened no matter how responsible you were.

Waiting for this day had been scary. But moving forward, I now realized, was scary too.

I arrived home from college a few days before Thanksgiving in 1985. I opened the front door and crossed the living room, its raggedy gold shag carpet a sad welcome mat. The sound of the TV blaring from the family room told me that's where I would find everyone.

"Hello?" I called out as I passed through the small kitchen, its flowered wallpaper and yellow-painted cupboards straining to look cheery, and entered the family room at the back of the house.

"Oh, Sharon!" Brian's smile lit up the room, and he enveloped me in a warm hug. My other siblings glanced up and said hello.

I looked over and saw my mother sleeping on the couch. It was the middle of the day.

"Hi, Mom."

She rose slowly, shuffled toward me, and sleepily kissed my cheek. She continued past me to her bedroom and shut the door, the creaky bedsprings accepting her weak and withered body. I stared after her.

"What's wrong with Mom?"

"She just sleeps a lot," was the response.

I was concerned enough to call Grampa, who convinced my mother to go to the emergency room. A simple blood test confirmed that she was suffering from end-stage renal failure—just like her mother before her—and she was in immediate need of dialysis. She was also eligible to begin the transplant evaluation process.

Except, she didn't.

She said she feared everything that could go wrong, which I suppose made sense, given her mother had died after a failed kidney transplant. But what if everything went right? Unfortunately, the longer she waited to get on the list, the more her health deteriorated, until she eventually became ineligible for a transplant. I was angry at my mother for giving up and for emotionally abandoning her children, who still needed her.

By early 1995, my mother's health was rapidly declining. She spent her days sleeping or glued to the TV watching the O.J. Simpson trial. Still, her lack of energy did not stop her from attending Pete's and my wedding in June.

Her seafoam-green dress and apricot blazer—which, she had proudly announced to wedding guests, she bought from Marshall's—perfectly matched my sisters' peach tea-length bridesmaids dresses. With my father gone, I had asked my mother to "walk" me down the aisle. Now wheelchair-bound, my mother clasped my hand as I walked alongside, a step ahead of the family friend rolling her down the aisle. Her hand was bony but soft and small. Arriving at the altar, my mother gave my hand a gentle squeeze before letting go, her prematurely aged face smiling faintly up at me.

I looked at my mother, familiar and yet a stranger. This was the same woman who chaperoned my Girl Scout camping trips, who played "Für Elise" on the piano before bedtime with her long, graceful fingers, who'd grinned conspiratorially when she let me play hooky from school to bake cookies and watch movies. This woman who looked like Jackie Kennedy on her wedding day in her loden green dress and matching pillbox hat—standing next to my boyish father, looking dapper in a suit and fedora in front of a late-1950s Cadillac—waving her white-gloved hand to the camera. This woman who was recently mistaken for my grandmother, her disease and its treatment having taken a horrible toll on her body.

I leaned over to give her a kiss.

"Your father would be so proud of you," she whispered in my ear, her voice barely audible. I was stunned to hear her talk about my father in a positive way. I choked back a tear as she was wheeled away. During the reading of the Gospel, I glanced over and saw her sitting peacefully with her eyes closed. Later, my sister remarked how our mother had fallen asleep during the ceremony, but I disagreed. "I think she was praying."

Two days later, my mother entered the hospital, where she died a month later from end-stage renal failure at the age of fifty-seven.

When it had become clear back in April that Evan was well on his way to recovery, I applied for a job at the Aspen Institute, a global nonprofit organization founded after World War II to tackle society's most pressing issues in an effort to ensure a free, just, and equitable society. They had a program area dedicated to two-generation solutions to lifting families out of poverty, aptly named Ascend.

Ascend had been a partner in the National Governors Association's two-generation initiative, and they were looking to hire a senior impact officer to help their Fellows—leaders in business, academia, government, and nonprofit sectors—create, implement, and document the impacts of their action plans for improving outcomes for children and families in their communities. I had actually gotten butterflies in my stomach when I read the job announcement to Pete, who agreed the job was a perfect fit for me. Due to COVID, Ascend had shifted from in-person to remote work, which meant that as long as I had a phone, a computer, and the internet, I could work safely from home.

But now, five months later, I had come to accept that I was not physically able to work full-time. I was deeply disappointed and terribly frustrated that I couldn't push through my fatigue and brain fog to take advantage of this wonderful opportunity. But I didn't want to make a commitment that I couldn't keep.

As I typed the email to Ascend withdrawing my application for the senior impact officer position, I thought of Evan and how hard it was for him not wanting to go anywhere or do anything because he never knew how he was going to feel. How he must have felt, *wanting* to complete his schoolwork, *wanting* to see his friends, *wanting* to take the multitude of pills every day—but simply unable to.

Unexpectedly, I thought of my parents. My father, denied the opportunity to be the dad he had wanted to be by the shackles of alcohol and the isolation of divorce. My mother, struggling to take care of six children while battling depression, kidney failure, and poverty. I finally had a glimmer of understanding of what my parents must have gone through. They loved us kids, they wanted the best for us, but they simply couldn't overcome their crumbling relationship, their fall into poverty, or their declining physical and mental health.

A feeling of shame washed over me as I realized how unfair it was for me to expect them to just snap out of it after their divorce. I had a new respect for how difficult it must have been for them, how it wasn't simply about personal responsibility or perseverance. My chest began to ache as I felt the enormity of their pain, no doubt wanting to do right by us kids but simply unable to. The deeply buried anger I had previously harbored toward my parents began to dissipate like the morning mist on a warm lake and was replaced by an all-consuming sorrow.

Chapter 31

October 2020

A strong breeze ruffled my hair and caused my skin to prickle as I scanned the layout of the brewery grounds atop the Blue Ridge Mountains, looking for seating that could accommodate eighteen family members. I was drawn to the outer perimeter, which provided a glorious view of the Loudoun Valley's patchwork of farmland unobstructed by other patrons, but I settled on a location closer to the entrance, which was less crowded and more accessible for Pete's aging parents than the expansive green lawn and its obstacle course of squealing children and dogs of all breeds, temperaments, and energy levels. I gestured to Pete, and he nodded, our unspoken language indicating that we agreed this was the best spot for celebrating Evan's twenty-first birthday.

Stay-at-home orders had been rescinded, but we were still hesitant to return to large family birthday parties held indoors. Meeting at a brewery and celebrating outdoors—making sure that everyone had tested negative on the newly available COVID saliva test beforehand—was the perfect solution.

Pete, Matthew, and Evan had just finished moving two picnic tables together when Pete's parents arrived. On their heels was Pete's sister, Alyssa, her husband, and our three rowdy nephews, now nine, seven, and four-and-a-half. With one fell swoop that would be the envy of any parent—or magician, for that matter—Alyssa shook open a tablecloth and flung it on the splintered wood table top with one hand, then placed the oblong Tupperware container holding homemade cupcakes on the neatly covered table with the other.

"Evan!" the trio of terror called, clinging to him tightly. They were thrilled to see Evan at family gatherings, still appearing somewhat surprised at his presence after years of missed holidays and birthday celebrations. Matthew feigned jealousy, and the boys turned their attention to him, running after him and toppling him onto the soft grass in a pig pile.

The sound of roughhousing used to cause my back to stiffen, anticipating the inevitable howl of pain when things went a little too far. But now, I was just glad to see Evan laughing again, and I was grateful for being able to spend time with our extended family for the first time since COVID had hit.

I looked over at Pete's mother, who was trying to get the boys to settle down while Pete's father was telling his wife to just let the kids play. A wave of melancholy hit me, wondering what kind of grandparents my parents would have been. Wondering what their lives would have been like had they lived into their sixties and beyond. If my father had sought help for his drinking, he might have found a job, been able to pay child support, remained in our lives, and avoided a horrific, untimely death. If my mother had been able to afford those CPA classes, she might have found a job with health insurance, escaped poverty, and maybe—just maybe—she could have been talked into seeing a doctor before her kidneys failed.

If only . . . at once a prayer and an acknowledgment that it was impossible to unwind the hands of time.

"Yay, Evan!" someone shouted, and I looked up to see Evan approaching us, precariously clutching four beers, a big smile on his face. Suddenly, he stumbled on a knotty root, his eyes widening in alarm as he tried to regain his balance and keep the beers from spilling. Amid cries of "Watch out!" from family members and gasps from onlookers, I just laughed. After four years of vigilant watchfulness trying to discern Evan's symptoms from each body movement and facial expression, I could tell a fake stumble from a real one. I also knew that Evan was always up for a gag—anything to make people laugh.

Evan handed the three red Solo cups dripping with spilled beer to Pete, Matthew, and me, and kept the pint glass emblazoned with the brewery logo for himself. He recounted how the bartender proofed him and, upon realizing it was his twenty-first birthday, wished him a happy birthday and handed him the commemorative glass filled to the rim with Evan's choice of adult beverage.

"Cheers!" everyone toasted.

Evan beamed as seventeen family members sang "Happy Birthday" in as many keys.

I regarded my twenty-one-year-old college freshman. In that moment, I realized that pushing Evan had never been about keeping pace with his peers. It wasn't even about falling behind. I now knew that in trying to help Evan, I had been nurturing my own fears of being stuck and that my efforts to control him—to push him to take his medicine, do his schoolwork, to see his friends—were really just my desperate attempts to prevent him from feeling stuck, growing despondent, and giving up hope. Like my parents did.

Lying in bed that night, I stared at the popcorn ceiling as Pete quietly snored next to me. I heard teasing and faint laughter through the heating vent, letting me know that Matthew and Evan were still up, playing video games in the basement. A breeze caressed my face, and I turned my head toward the open window, the sheer curtains billowing slightly. I breathed in the cool night air and listened to the wind gently rattle the shutters. Burrowing more deeply into my down comforter, I exhaled a contented sigh and closed my eyes, overcome by a sense of peace and happiness. I whispered a prayer of gratitude, for I knew that ordinary days like today were actually extraordinary, and they should not be taken for granted.

Chapter 32

Winter 2020–2021

The week after my September tele-visit with Dr. Assefi, I received a call from the transplant center. A soft-spoken woman introduced herself as my pretransplant intake coordinator and provided an overview of the transplant evaluation process, which required that I provide an in-depth medical history and undergo a number of tests to determine if I was healthy enough to withstand transplant surgery.

I subsequently received calls from the transplant surgeon to discuss the transplant evaluation process in greater depth and to answer any questions I had, the transplant social worker to assess my psychosocial readiness for a transplant—asking about my concerns and sources of social and emotional support—and the transplant financial coordinator to review my insurance coverage.

Last fall, when I was convinced that a transplant was imminent, Pete and I had carefully reviewed the health insurance options offered by his company and selected the plan that would minimize our out-of-pocket costs. We had learned that the average cost for a kidney transplant in the US was just over $400,000, so our twenty percent co-pay would be a whopping $80,000. Still, I shuddered to think how much more we would have had to pay if the Affordable Care Act hadn't prohibited insurers from charging higher premiums—or denying coverage altogether—for individuals with preexisting conditions. And we were one of the lucky ones, I reminded myself. At least we could afford the exorbitant cost of this life-saving surgery. My heart ached for others who weren't as fortunate.

A week before Thanksgiving, I began the medical tests required as part of the transplant evaluation process. I underwent a series of blood tests to check for certain viruses and to see how my immune system, kidneys, and other organs were functioning. I submitted blood and tissue samples that would be used to find a donor match. A chest X-ray looked for infection, disease, and other abnormalities of my lungs; an abdominal CT scan checked for tumors and other internal injuries or damage; and a mammogram, pap smear, and colonoscopy checked for cancer. The search for possible abnormalities in my heart included an echocardiogram (an ultrasound of the heart's chambers, valves, and pumping), an electrocardiogram (a test of the heart's electrical system), and a cardiac stress test (to assess whether my heart was strong enough to undergo transplant surgery).

I dreaded the stress test. I had had two cardiac stress tests done in my forties when I had felt an irregular heartbeat and lightheadedness, similar to but not as severe as the episode I had nearly three years ago that landed me in the emergency room. Designed to see how the heart responded when it was working its hardest—for a woman my age, that meant 164 beats per minute—a cardiac stress test involved walking on a treadmill that gradually increased in speed with intermittent periods of rest. A doctor monitored the ECG readout while a nurse stood behind you, placing gentle pressure on your lower back to keep you moving forward as you tired.

I had thought nothing could be worse than the fear of flying off the back of a treadmill as my legs turned to jelly and my lungs threatened to explode . . . until I had to do the cardiac stress test through my N95 mask. As predicted, COVID cases had skyrocketed since the fall, and by early January 2021, there were 115,000 new hospitalizations and 26,000 COVID-related deaths each week, both record highs. As much as I dreaded wearing a mask for this already challenging medical test, I dreaded becoming infected with COVID and becoming ineligible for a kidney transplant even more.

The day of the stress test arrived. It was mid-January, and the sky was clear and the sun shone brightly—which brightened my spirits but didn't entirely eliminate my trepidation. Pete had offered to take the day off from work to drive me, but I told him I would be fine. Although I was comfortable being vulnerable around my husband, I didn't want to feel vulnerable, which is how I would have felt had I allowed him to dote on me. Besides, simply offering to help was enough to lift my spirits.

Soon after checking in, a tall nurse in blue scrubs and a pristine white N95 mask called my name, guided me to the test room, and instructed me to change into a gown. Moments later, she returned, along with the physician who would be overseeing the test. The doctor introduced herself and described what I could expect and how long the test would take. She was a petite woman with a kind, confident voice that was only partially muffled by her N95 mask, and she reminded me of Dr. Afrooz. I willed myself to relax as the nurse connected the electrodes to my chest and arms and started the treadmill.

I managed the walking pace with ease. The speed increased, and I began to breathe a little harder. The speed increased even more, and a small incline was added. My legs were really working now, but I managed to keep up. The treadmill sped up again, and this time, I had to almost run to stay centered on the belt. I felt a gentle hand on my back and was both relieved and terrified that, without the nurse's help, I would have sailed off the back by now.

With each breath of the warm, carbon dioxide–rich air inside my mask, my extremities tingled, my vision tunneled, and I felt increasingly lightheaded. I wanted desperately to quit, to give up. To rest. The nurse's cheers of "You can do this!" and "A break is coming up in ten seconds!"—and the knowledge that my eligibility for a kidney transplant hung in the balance—were the only things that kept me going.

The doctor counted down the final seconds, congratulated me on completing the test, then helped me off the treadmill. My knees buckled as the nurse led me to the examination table, where I immediately lay down and pulled the mask from my face, gulping down the cool air. Despite my nearly single focus on breathing, I watched the doctor, trying to discern from her facial expressions as she scanned the ECG readout whether or not I had passed the test.

I began to worry, irrationally, that the longer I lay there collapsed in a heap, the more likely they'd declare me ineligible for a transplant. I forced myself to sit up, but a wave of dizziness and my fading peripheral vision caused me to lie back down. The nurse brought me water and helped me take sips while the doctor listened to my heart with her stethoscope. They both were telling me I did a great job.

The following day, I learned that the cardiac stress test result was normal.

I pulled out the transplant evaluation checklist that my pretransplant intake coordinator had sent me back in September and checked off "cardiac stress test" with a flourish. The bright-blue checkmark matched those I had placed next to CT scan, chest X-ray, mammogram, pap, echocardiogram, electrocardiogram, and colonoscopy over the past three months. The checklist looked like a winning coverall Bingo card, and I smiled.

Chapter 33

June 2021

It was odd. Some days, I felt fine—rested, mentally sharp—and I went on with my day. Other days, like today, I was listless and couldn't maintain a train of thought. Sometimes coffee, a shower, or a walk would deliver the needed boost of energy and wash away the cobwebs. But increasingly, they didn't.

Today's symptoms were overwhelming. Emerging from the basement an hour earlier after throwing in a load of laundry, I had to bend over, hands on my knees, to catch my breath, heaving as if I'd just hiked up a mountain. My peripheral vision began to fade, and I quickly collapsed onto the sofa until the tingling lightheadedness of having almost fainted dissipated.

Despite my difficulty breathing, I didn't suspect COVID. I continued to avoid public spaces, and after months of chasing the limited supply of COVID vaccines across Northern Virginia's health departments and pharmacies, I had finally received the long-awaited vaccinations in March and April.

No, this was something else entirely, I feared.

A few days later, my pretransplant intake coordinator called for my monthly check-in. After confirming that I had received the recommended two doses of the long-awaited COVID vaccine, she ran through the usual list of questions: Have you had any illness or hospitalizations in the past month? Do you still have a support person who can take you to and from clinic appointments?

When she asked how I was feeling, I told her that I was fuzzy-headed and short of breath and that I couldn't make it through the day without a nap. Although I wasn't due for my quarterly blood work for another month, she urged me to get tested immediately, reminding me that once my kidney functioning dipped below twenty percent, I would be placed on the national transplant list, where I would remain even if my subsequent functioning rose above twenty percent.

I went to LabCorp the following morning, and by the time Pete had arrived home from work later that afternoon, I had the results.

My single kidney was functioning at nineteen percent.

Although the results signaled a decline, I was elated. I could finally get on the transplant list and, God willing, avoid dialysis.

"Pete!" I called him over to look at the test results on my phone. "Am I reading this right?"

But it was clear as a sunny day, the bolded 19.0. Pete nodded and gave me a hug.

One week later, on Pete's and my twenty-sixth wedding anniversary, I received the official letter notifying me that I had been placed on the kidney transplant list.

"It's good to know we have a backup," Pete had whispered into my ear.

Chapter 34

June 2021

A kidney from a deceased donor was my second option. My first option was Pete.

Soon after I completed the transplant evaluation process earlier this year, Pete began testing to be a live donor.

We knew we had the same blood type, which was the first step in assessing biological compatibility. Pete then filled out a detailed medical history, which did not uncover any medical conditions that would prevent him from donating. We passed the crossmatch test—meaning that the antibodies in my blood did not react negatively to the antibodies in Pete's blood. We passed the human leukocyte antigen (HLA) tissue typing test, matching on all six antigens (substances in the body that triggered an immune response in the presence of foreign tissue) identified as the most important for organ transplantation.

In other words, Pete was a perfect match.

I was deeply grateful for Pete in my life. He was solid and predictable. He was sweet and funny. He held it together when I fell apart. A perfect match, indeed.

Chapter 35

August 2021

We stood outside the former farmhouse, its white clapboard siding brilliant against the deep-blue sky. Earlier in the day, Pete, Matthew, and I had helped Evan move into this four-bedroom duplex that he would share with three other Virginia Tech students.

I was surprised at my stamina—I spent hours moving boxes and small items, needing only a few short breaks to catch my breath and drink some water. It was as if my body had adjusted to my recent drop in kidney functioning and had established a new equilibrium. A new normal.

We had just returned from a celebratory lunch at one of the boys' favorite restaurants in Blacksburg, El Rodeo—or "Elrod's," as the students called it. We had toasted Evan with a round of margaritas, and I had snapped a picture of him raising his glass—his smile bright, his eyes twinkling—and I knew exactly where this photo would go: over the mantel, in the center of his school pictures that currently stood empty. It may not be his high school senior picture, but it still portrayed a key milestone on the cusp of new beginnings.

When it was time for Pete, Matthew, and me to head home, we each went to hug Evan goodbye. Playfully stumbling over each other, our individual hugs merged into one big embrace. I was the last to let go, releasing Evan from my grip and cupping his face in my hands. His eyes, damp with tears, met mine.

"This," I said simply. "This is what I wanted for you, what I knew lay ahead for you. This is what you worked so hard for, and I'm so proud of you!"

Evan gave me another hug, his strong arms pulling me close.

"Thank you for everything," he whispered, his voice cracking. "I love you."

"I love you too," I said, giving him an extra squeeze before letting go.

Pete offered to drive home, and I nodded. Between the tears clouding my eyes and the pit of sadness in my stomach, I knew I was in no condition to get behind the wheel. I sat in the back seat, ceding the front passenger seat to Matthew and his long legs. I looked out the back window and saw Evan on the front porch, standing tall like a soldier at attention: his chin up, chest out, and shoulders back. Only his downturned smile conveyed a sadness that was otherwise masked by his confident posture. I waved goodbye and continued to do so until the road dipped down the rolling hill, eclipsing my view, and Evan disappeared.

Epilogue

Fall 2021

I reclined on the antigravity lounge chair in our backyard, listening to the symphony of bird calls, lawn mowers, barking dogs, and the faint hum of traffic, watching the feathery cirrus clouds slowly lengthen across the sky like silky hair being brushed straight. I drew in deep, slow breaths and reached for my ever-present water bottle.

I watched the trees sway lazily in the cool afternoon breeze, their leaves a bounty of green with scattered shades of yellow, orange, and red. Winter would be on us before we knew it, with its slower pace and much of nature enjoying an extended rest.

Evan was enjoying Virginia Tech and had already made a few friends in his psychology classes. Matthew decided to move to Phoenix early the next year and share an apartment with an online gaming friend. The chance to live in a different part of the country appealed to Matthew, especially after having been cooped up at home for the past eighteen months due to the pandemic.

Pete was back to work full-time, and although they were no longer required to wear masks, he continued to do so in meetings and when in close proximity to others. He did not want to jeopardize my health and risk my eligibility for a transplant. These days, I was the one reminding him to drink more water, teasing him that he was incubating my kidney, and I didn't want a dud. Most days, he'd laugh at my attempts at humor, but some days, I could see the concern peek through his smiling eyes.

I began working again in September, consulting remotely for ten hours a week for Ascend. I was looking forward to spending the next eighteen months leading a group of experts in developing a research agenda for the two-generation field. As I saw former colleagues on social media continuing to advance in their careers, I sometimes wondered wistfully what might have been if I didn't have chronic kidney disease. But then I thought of Evan and how Lyme disease may have slowed him down, but it didn't stop him. He just had to find his own pace and his own path—just like I had to find mine. If Evan could not only survive but thrive after a chronic illness, then so could I.

My kidney functioning was holding steady—in fact, my single kidney's capacity had increased slightly to twenty percent in July. I was immensely grateful that my pretransplant intake coordinator suggested that I get tested back in June. *What were the odds that my functioning would dip to nineteen percent during that brief window?* Sure, I was relying on Pete's kidney for a transplant, but I knew that illness and disease could strike at any time.

I thought of my mother. I was now the same age that she was when she died. It's an odd feeling, knowing that you've outlived your parents. Although I know they died young, it feels like I somehow cheated death and was now living on borrowed time. A dark thought, perhaps, but one that made life feel even more precious.

I had no way of knowing when I would need a kidney. Dr. Assefi said it depended on the seriousness of my symptoms and would likely be when my functioning reached between six and ten percent capacity. But would that be in one year? Five years? I had no idea. For someone who spent her life planning, strategizing, setting goals, and working hard to achieve them, I now found myself hesitant to make plans for the future.

As a cloud eclipsed the sun, I realized that I had spent so much of my adult life resenting my parents for what they couldn't provide that I hadn't appreciated all they taught me. From my mother, I learned the importance of pursuing a career, of believing in something bigger than myself, and in having faith in dire situations. From my father, I learned that strong family relationships were not just enjoyable, they were vital to our very survival.

I'd also learned from Evan over the past five years. I learned that pauses don't have to mean stagnancy and despair. They can be an opportunity to slow down, to reassess life priorities, and to find gratitude in all that was going right rather than perseverating over all that was going—or could go—wrong. Pauses, I now knew, could be life-giving, providing a needed rest and even an opportunity for growth, like plants that lay dormant in winter, conserving their energy until better growing conditions allowed them to flourish in the spring.

But most of all, I learned that, like the spring after a dark and dreary winter or the burst of sunlight after a storm, the light always returned.

References

Abigail Dumes, "What the 'Lyme Wars' Can Teach Us About COVID-19 and How to Find Common Ground in the School Reopening Debate," *The Conversation*, August 19, 2021, https://theconversation.com/what-the-lyme-wars-can-teach-us-about-covid-19-and-how-to-find-common-ground-in-the-school-reopening-debate-165375/.

"About Lyme Disease: Overview," Centers for Disease Control and Prevention, August 26, 2024, https://www.cdc.gov/lyme/about/index.html/.

Caroline Hopkins, "Why Lyme Disease Symptoms Go Away Quickly for Some and Last Years for Others," NBC News, May 14, 2023, https://www.nbcnews.com/health/health-news/lyme-disease-symptoms-recover-fast-others-not-rcna83340/.

"Evaluation for Kidney Transplant," National Kidney Foundation, https://www.kidney.org/kidney-topics/evaluation-kidney-transplant/.

H. W. Longfellow, "Henry Wadsworth Longfellow," Maine Historical Society, https://www.hwlongfellow.org/.

Loraine Fick, reviewed by Minesh Khatri, MD, "What Is Hypersensitivity Pneumonitis?" *WebMD*, September 18, 2022, https://www.webmd.com/lung/hypersensitivity-pneumonitis-overview/.

Marcelo Campos, MD, "Lyme Disease: Resolving the 'Lyme Wars,'" Harvard Health Publishing, June 18, 2018, https://www.health.harvard.edu/blog/lyme-disease-resolving-the-lyme-wars-2018061814071/.

Michael Specter, "The Lyme Wars," republished on White Oak Medical from *The New Yorker*, April 2016, https://whiteoakmedical.com/2016/04/01/lyme-wars/.

Nicola McFadzean, *The Lyme Diet: Nutritional Strategies for Healing from Lyme Disease* (New York, NY: BioMed Publishing Group, 2010).

Richard Horowitz, *Why Can't I Get Better? Solving the Mystery of Lyme and Chronic Disease* (New York, NY: St. Martin's Griffin, 2013).

Richard Horowitz, *How Can I Get Better? An Action Plan for Treating Resistant Lyme & Chronic Disease* (New York, NY: St. Martin's Griffin, 2017).

"Rocky Mountain Spotted Fever," Harvard Health Publishing, December 29, 2021, https://www.health.harvard.edu/a_to_z/rocky-mountain-spotted-fever-a-to-z.

Notes

1. Mayo Clinic Staff, "Aspergillosis," Mayo Clinic, January 6, 2022, https://www.mayoclinic.org/diseases-conditions/aspergillosis/symptoms-causes/syc-20369619.
2. Loraine Fick, reviewed by Minesh Khatri, MD, "What Is Hypersensitivity Pneumonitis?," WebMD, September 18, 2022, https://www.webmd.com/lung/hypersensitivity-pneumonitis-overview/.
3. "About Lyme Disease," Centers for Disease Control and Prevention, August 26, 2024, https://www.cdc.gov/lyme/about/index.html/.
4. "Signs and Symptoms of Untreated Lyme Disease," Centers for Disease Control and Prevention, October 30, 2024, https://www.cdc.gov/lyme/signs-symptoms/index.html.
5. Richard Horowitz, *Why Can't I Get Better? Solving the Mystery of Lyme & Chronic Disease* (New York, NY: St. Martin's Press, 2013).
6. Richard Horowitz, *How Can I Get Better? An Action Plan for Treating Resistant Lyme & Chronic Disease* (New York, NY: St. Martin's Griffin Press, 2017).
7. Nicola McFadzean, *The Lyme Diet: Nutritional Strategies for Healing from Lyme Disease* (South Lake Tahoe, CA: BioMed Publishing Group, 2010).
8. "About Histoplasmosis," Centers for Disease Control and Prevention, April 24, 2024, accessed February 2017, https://www.cdc.gov/histoplasmosis/about/index.html/.

9. "Clinical and Laboratory Diagnosis for Rocky Mountain Spotted Fever," Centers for Disease Control and Prevention, May 15, 2024, https://www.cdc.gov/rocky-mountain-spotted-fever/hcp/diagnosis-testing/index.html/.
10. Anthony J Bleyer, et al. "Outcomes of Patient Self-Referral for the Diagnosis of Several Rare Inherited Kidney Diseases," *Genetics in Medicine*, 22(1): 42-149, 2019, DOI: 10.1038/s41436-019-0617.
11. Jn 14:27 New Revised Standard Version Updated Edition.
12. Julian of Norwich, *Revelations of Divine Love*, https://www.gutenberg.org/files/52958/52958-h/52958-h.htm/.
13. Lk 12:25 New American Standard Bible Updated Edition.
14. Anne Lamott, *Plan B: Further Thoughts on Faith* (New York, NY: Riverhead Books, 2006).

About the Author

Sharon McGroder is a social science researcher with publications on antipoverty and family strengthening programs in academic journals, including *Child Development, Journal of Marriage and Family*, and *The Journal of Prevention & Intervention in the Community*. She received a BS in political science and an MS in public policy analysis from the University of Rochester and a PhD in human development and family studies from Pennsylvania State University. Sharon was recently named executive director of the Rare Kidney Disease Foundation (www.rarekidney.org). She lives with her family and their dog outside Washington, DC.

www.ingramcontent.com/pod-product-compliance
Lightning Source LLC
Chambersburg PA
CBHW060522080526
44586CB00012B/577